Countering Colonization

Countering Colonization

Native American Women and Great Lakes Missions, 1630–1900

CAROL DEVENS

UNIVERSITY OF CALIFORNIA PRESS
Berkeley   Los Angeles   Oxford

E
78
.67
D48
1992

University of California Press
Berkeley and Los Angeles, California

University of California Press, Ltd.
Oxford, England

© 1992 by
The Regents of the University of California

Library of Congress Cataloging-in-Publication Data

Devens, Carol.
  Countering colonization: Native American women and Great Lakes missions,
1630–1900 / Carol Devens.
    p. cm.
  Includes bibliographical references and index.
  ISBN 0-520-07557-9 (alk. paper)
    1. Indians of North America—Great Lakes Region—Women. 2. Women—Great
Lakes Region—History. 3. Sex role—Great Lakes Region—History. 4. Indians of
North America—Great Lakes Region—Missions. 5. Indians of North America—
Canada, Eastern—Women. 6. Women—Canada, Eastern—History. 7. Sex role—
Canada, Eastern—History. 8. Indians of North America—Canada, Eastern—
Missions. I. Title.
E78.G7D48   1992
977′.00497′082—dc20   91-4791
                                                                                CIP

Printed in the United States of America
9 8 7 6 5 4 3 2 1

An earlier version of Chapter 1 appeared as "Separate Confrontations: Gender as a
Factor in Indian Adaptation to European Colonization in New France," *American
Quarterly* 38, no. 3 (Bibliography, 1986): 461–80.

To Lee and Aric

Contents

Maps

Acknowledgments

My greatest debt is to Lee Devens, whose love, friendship, and support have helped me to complete this study, and to our son, Aric, whose very existence has changed my personal view of history. Through the years the encouragement of my parents, Margaret and William Green, and of Virginia Devens has bolstered my spirits as well.

My other debts are many. Valarie Ziegler has been a friend and sister in ways beyond measure. Rande and Janet Aaronson and Susan Kus have given me the assurance and caring that are so crucial to any endeavor of this sort and which have meant more to me than they may realize. I also appreciate the cheerful friendship of Laura Brener, Paul Clemens, Carol Danehower, Kathy Jones, and Kenneth Goings.

Ernie Isaacs and Charles Roberts at California State University, Sacramento, introduced me to the excitement as well as the methodology of social history and effectively diverted me from a career in law—many thanks. The members of the Department of History at Rutgers University contributed many helpful suggestions to the dissertation out of which this book developed. Nancy Oestreich Lurie of the Milwaukee Public Museum provided a much-needed anthropological perspective. A Woodrow Wilson National Fellowship Foundation Doctoral Dissertation Fellowship in Women's Studies underwrote part of the research for this project, and I am grateful for the support. Rhodes College also provided two Faculty Development Endowment grants.

I wish to extend my thanks as well to the archivists of both the Houghton Library at Harvard University and the Methodist Archives at Drew University. Joyce Ruth Jessup and Denise Vaughn typed successive drafts of the manuscripts. Finally, I express my appreciation to the editorial staff of the University of California Press for their thoughtful work and patience.

Introduction

The history of nonliterate peoples is difficult to commit to paper. Those of us who attempt to do so are forced to depend on and cope with the whims and biases of long-departed observers, in addition to struggling with our own. In the long course of completing this project I often was asked, and sometimes asked myself, why I focused on peoples whom many deem culturally, chronologically, and ideologically remote from the mainstream.

This book stems from three concerns. One is to bring Native American women in from the margins of written history, to acknowledge in the Western record the place they have always held in their own cultures. The second has to do with colonization as a process, with the dynamics of the meeting and ongoing interaction of indigenous and alien peoples and the role that gender plays in this unfolding. Finally, the book grew out of my discontent with anthropological studies of Native Americans that, in describing social relations and ideology, often overlooked both historical process and gender.

The history of the struggle to colonize North America is, it seems, one that those of us who belong to the dominant society know almost intrinsically—it is part and parcel of our childhoods even if it is not our personal heritage. As children, we cut Pilgrim hats and feathered headbands from construction paper and turn the traced outlines of our hands into turkeys. We learn of ordeals, of perseverance, and of success. The chronicle of "settlement" that is taught us is a story of men: brave men who came, saw, and conquered both a vast wilderness and other, savage, men. Bradford, Winthrop, White, Cortés, de Soto, Champlain, even Squanto and Powhatan—the very texts are rosters redolent of rigor, strength, and valor. They are annals of masculine exploits and defeats in a brave New World uncomplicated by the presence of women.

Our childhood perspective, comforting in its clarity, is anchored both in the narratives of the conquerors and in those of the scholars who studied them. The European men who explored America came from cultures with political and socioeconomic systems shaped by an earlier feudal patriarchy, a social order rooted in a tradition of masculine authority and activity that presupposed feminine passivity and domesticity. Theirs was a world that could acknowledge women as actors only when simultaneously depicting them as anomalies. Given the worldview of the explorers, Native American women could not have appeared as participants in the drama of colonization except in the most insignificant of roles. Women were drudges, squaws unsuited for shouldering the burdens of conquest or resistance, bystanders in the trials and tribulations of a male world.

Generations of scholars, molded by many of the same assumptions, accepted the views of those contemporary observers who minimized Native American women's roles. And so history presented us with a genderless scenario in which whites battled Indians, who sometimes capitulated and sometimes fought back. We remained unaware of the intricacies of interaction with an alien culture or of the complexity of the impact of colonization, of concerns that extended far beyond the stark issues of victory or defeat. Lacking a clear sense that these "Indian" men were more than recipients of a tragic (or to some, well-deserved) fate, we did not recognize that they were members of communities facing a myriad of decisions on how to deal with European intruders while still remaining within the tribal universe.

In the wake of anticolonial movements over the past four decades, however, historians and anthropologists have begun to reevaluate colonization both as a process and as an experience—to deconstruct colonial systems and propose new models for understanding the dynamics of colonization. The alternate frameworks that result allow for the actions of all parties by analyzing not only how colonizers operated but also how indigenous peoples acted: when and why they resisted or accommodated the newcomers. Moreover, the new frameworks free us to examine what forces were at play when native peoples did not act of one accord, what factors motivated interest groups and determined their tactics. As Paula Gunn Allen has suggested in

The Sacred Hoop, colonization is more than a matter of economics; it involves peoples' values, how they view the universe and their place in it.[1]

One purpose of the present study is to consider how native communities perceived colonizers and how those perceptions influenced whether people presented a unified front or split into factions of accommodation and resistance. To this end, I have examined one aspect of the colonization process—the missions—and a series of discrete episodes within the missionary endeavor.[2] Missionaries, with their goals of converting and "civilizing" native peoples, were a vital part of colonization; they provided the ideological counterpart to economic and political manipulation and exploitation. In addition, their affiliation with missionary organizations required them to communicate both factual information and personal opinions to their superiors; thus they generated a body of material unparalleled by nongovernmental facets of the colonial system.

Given the above characterization of the male-oriented worldview of European and American colonizers, it may seem contradictory to depend on their accounts for knowledge about the significance of gender in their contact with Indians. Yet the sources belie the stance taken by their authors. Missionaries and other travelers related in detail (with a disapproval sometimes verging on horror) information on native women's status and autonomy, all the while diligently pointing out the barbarity of native sex roles. The disparities between indigenous gender relations and those fostered by missionaries at times had a decisive impact on native groups. The "mechanisms of colonization," as Allen suggests, are at the core of the antagonism that exists between women and men in American Indian communities.[3]

Because Ojibwa, Cree, and Montagnais-Naskapi communities of the Great Lakes and eastern subarctic encountered missionaries of several denominations from the early colonial period through the nineteenth century, a fact that allows us to look for larger patterns of response rather than focus on an isolated situation, these groups provide the focus of the study. When we look at the larger picture, at several centuries of contact, three patterns of response become evident. Although each community had as its primary concern the group's survival, how they attempted to assure it varied with the circumstances. The first two patterns involved united responses. In the first, whole communities expelled missionaries whom they viewed as threats to tribal lifeways and security. At other times, adverse economic conditions elicited a quiet, if grudging, accommodation to Christianity by the entire group. The third pattern, however, was a split response. When missions or economics affected women and men unevenly, communities divided along gender lines into factions that supported different approaches to dealing with changes disrupting their world.

In the earliest phase of missionization, seventeenth-century French Jesuits urged Indians to adopt a male-dominated nuclear family just as the demands of the fur trade were disrupting socioeconomic relationships. The resulting shift favored the productive activities of native men and caused rifts between males and females in a number of proselytized communities. In the nineteenth century, native people received Protestant missionaries in several different ways. In relatively isolated communities, whose economic basis remained sound enough to see no need for accommodating whites, missionaries found themselves rejected or ignored. But when evangelicals preached their combined gospel of assimilation and female domesticity in areas where the pressures of white settlement, economic and environmental stress, and native dislocation demanded that Indian males negotiate with the colonizers, the outcome was either general accommodation or a course of action that divided women and men.

By the late nineteenth century the latter pattern had become the norm. As men grew more receptive to introduced practices and values that they hoped would allow them to deal successfully with whites, women stood only to lose status and autonomy. Thus, whereas many men favored accommodation, women tended to stress "traditional" ways. As a consequence, asymmetrical, even antagonistic relations between the sexes eventually prevailed in many communities. This pattern clarifies the significance of gender in the colonization process. As importantly, however, it recasts classic ethnographic characterizations of the tension in gender relations: rather than being an "aboriginal" strain, fundamental to the social and ideological structures of Native American cultures, the friction between men and women is in fact the bitter fruit of colonization.

1

THE FIRST PATTERN
The Response to Jesuit Missions

"It is you women," charged the men of a Montagnais band in New France in 1640, " . . . who are the cause of all our misfortunes,—it is you who keep the demons among us. You do not urge to be baptized; you must not be satisfied to ask this favor only once from the Fathers, you must importune them. You are lazy about going to prayers; when you pass before the cross, you never salute it; you wish to be independent. Now know that you will obey your husbands."[1] Frustrated and angry, the men blamed women's commitment to traditional beliefs as the stumbling block to the community's well-being. This band of Cree-speaking people in the St. Lawrence region of Canada had been under French influence since a Jesuit missionary coaxed survivors of the 1639–40 smallpox epidemic to accompany him from their summer encampment at Trois Rivières to the St. Joseph mission at Sillery, established three years earlier. There the French had sheltered them, and resident Christian Indians soon demanded their conversion. The priest who recorded the above incident never mentioned if the women capitulated, but he did remark that at least one woman escaped into the forest rather than submit. The majority of men, apparently convinced that female independence and lack of interest in Christianity had divided the group, resolved that should she be captured, they would chain and starve her as punishment.[2]

There was more at stake in the conflict between the men and women at St. Joseph's, however, than the simple desire of male converts to find a scapegoat for their troubles. Indeed, the tensions in this community disclose the first pattern of response to colonization: gender-based perceptions of and reactions to Christianity and Western culture. Although this pattern may

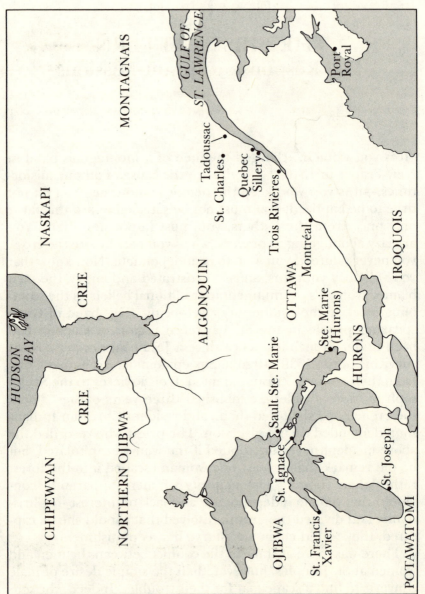

Jesuit Missions and Tribal Areas

not have typified all native peoples of New France, it was evident among many of the "domiciled" groups who are the focus of the present study. In their communities, a good number of men decided to adopt Catholicism and a sedentary life-style—thus, perhaps, reflecting a reassessment of the viability of the traditional system. Some scholars have argued that male converts, along with priests, brooked no opposition from women at the missions and succeeded in undermining women's status by 1640.[3] While there is little doubt that this was, indeed, the Christian neophytes' intention, the men's accusations make it clear that some women stubbornly resisted the imposition of both Christian values and gender roles well into the mission era.

The Jesuit mission to New France began in 1611 when Pierre Biard and Ennemond Massé arrived to proselytize the Abnaki in the vicinity of Port Royal. The mission, short-lived and fraught with misadventure, ended with the priests' capture by a Virginian expedition in 1613. Only in 1625 did Jesuits return to the colony, joining a small contingent of Recollets who had labored in their stead during the intervening years. Even so, the Jesuits did not successfully install their mission until 1632, for in 1629 English raiders carried away Jesuit and Recollet alike in the process of commandeering French settlements. When France regained its possessions in 1632, the Jesuits' moment had arrived: the drive to evangelize the *sauvages* of eastern Canada now began in earnest. The missionaries commenced with the Montagnais in the environs of the reopened Quebec parish and within the year had ventured to the trading post upriver at Trois Rivières; St. Joseph's at Sillery opened its palisaded doors to interested Montagnais and Algonquins in 1637.[4]

Throughout the remainder of the seventeenth century, bands of Cree, Ojibwa, and Algonquins settled in villages adjoining missions across New France, usually to secure protection from predatory enemy bands or to recuperate from the devastating epidemics that swept the area with morbid regularity. And occasionally Jesuits settled with them, hoping to make the villages home bases for future mission sites.

These Algonquian-speaking peoples occupied the land from Labrador to Lake Winnipeg.[5] The Ojibwa, Cree, and Montagnais-Naskapi based their economies primarily on hunting, fishing,

and gathering, although some more southerly groups of
Ojibwa practiced occasional horticulture. They also shared
many elements of material culture, social organization, and ritual beliefs and practices. These similarities allow us to consider
their interactions with Europeans as analogous without dis-
counting the discreet worldviews and lifeways of each group.
Such a regional approach makes it feasible to move beyond the
sometimes contrived and limited political delineations of tribes
and to look instead at the dynamics of colonization.[6] Because of
the many affinities in material culture and ideology, I will in-
clude some information on Ottawa and on Micmac of the
Gaspé Peninsula and Maritimes as well.

Reports, journals, and travel accounts from New France fur-
nish us with a large, if biased, portrait of the social organizations and belief systems of native communities in the early contact period.[7] Prominent in this profile is the sexual division that
permeated all aspects of the native peoples' world—in rituals,
the exercise of authority, productive and reproductive activities, spatial arrangements, and food distribution—and profoundly influenced how women and men faced the vicissitudes
of daily living. Each sex played an integral yet autonomous role
in the social and productive unit. Males and females had complementary functions that seldom overlapped, though they
might be overlooked temporarily when necessary, as during a
spouse's illness. As Paul Le Jeune, superior of the reopened
missions, noted of the Montagnais in 1632,

> the women know what they are to do, and the men also; and one
> never meddles with the work of the other. The men make the
> frames of their canoes, and the women sew the bark with willow
> withes or similar wood. The men shape the wood of the raquettes
> [snowshoes], and the women do the sewing on them. Men go hunt-
> ing, and kill the animals; and the women go after them, skin them,
> and clean the hides.[8]

"To live among us without a wife," one man later explained, "is
to live without help, without home, and to be always wan-
dering."[9]

Ritual practices and beliefs complemented the separation of
responsibility and authority. Men and their rituals focused on

the bush. Although males actively participated in camp life, their primary productive role was hunting large game and fur-bearers such as moose, caribou, bear, beaver, and deer. A man's authority and value to his group arose from his contributions as a hunter, and the respect tendered him rested on his skills. Success in the chase depended on the cooperation of animal spirits and the guidance of supernatural "helpers" gained through vision quests, dreaming, or divination. Men moved between the bush and the camp yet governed neither, for animal spirits "owned" the bush, and women controlled the camp.[10] With the exception of warring and divination, males' activities as hunters required minimal cooperative effort; instead men generally worked alone or in very small groups, a degree of physical isolation from the group forced upon them by their responsibilities. For Cree men working in the deep, powdery snow of the northern forests and muskeg, as for Ojibwa and Algonquin men of the Great Lakes, hunting meant absence from the camp for days, perhaps weeks, as they tracked game or checked traps.[11] A hunter's relationship with the supernaturals vital to the chase, too, was a highly individual one, which he was compelled to maintain on his own, even though rituals designed to placate animal spirits, such as returning beaver bones to water, were observed by the whole community to ensure their continued well-being and full stomachs.[12]

Women usually worked apart from men, either within the commensal unit or in groups, and the communal nature of their work allowed them regular contact with one another. They fished and hunted small game, such as rabbit, marten, and birds, in the vicinity of the camp, providing a good portion of the daily diet. In the mixed conifer-deciduous forests of Wisconsin and Minnesota, dotted with numerous lakes and rivers, women of the small, autonomous bands of Southwestern Ojibwa gathered nuts, berries, and fruits and tapped sugar maples, and in the fall both sexes harvested wild rice. The women of all groups also controlled the distribution of meat; once the men reported the kill, it became the women's property to butcher and process as they saw fit.[13] After spending the winter of 1633–34 in the bush with a Montagnais band, Paul Le Jeune described this exchange with amazement: "Men leave the arrangement of the household to the women, without interfering with them; they cut, and decide, and give away [meat] as they please, without making the husband angry."[14] A woman's distribution of meat to families within the group established her autonomy and her authority to control food while reinforcing a sense of community and interdependence among households.[15]

Women were responsible for processing hides—scraping, stretching, and rubbing them with brains or grease—to be used as furs or made into shirts, leggings, parkas, moccasins, and other items of clothing; and they fashioned animal bones into awls, needles, ladles, and other tools (with the exception of bear and beaver skulls and feet, which received special ritual treatment). Men then received these items in exchange for the meat they provided. Women also controlled the assignment of living space and the selection of campsites.

Raising and training children occupied an important place in women's activities; after weaning at the age of two or three a child's care became a communal effort in which all women participated. Children were cherished, and they also were needed for the parents' support in old age. Births apparently were carefully planned and spaced, through abstinence and possibly through the use of abortion. "The father and mother draw the morsel from the mouth if the child asks for it," commented Nicolas Denys. "They love their children greatly." A Jesuit observer similarly remarked, "The Savages love their children above all things. They are like the Monkeys—they choke them by embracing them too closely."[16]

Women kept most ritual activities, like their practical activities, separate from those of men. Shamanistic rituals, such as the shaking tent or divination, were performed by both sexes. For example, Le Jeune described a woman performing the shaking tent ritual: "At the three Rivers [Trois Rivières], a Juggler having called the Manitou, or some other Genius, and not having succeeded in making him come, a woman entered and began to shake the house and to sing and cry so loudly, that she caused the devil to come."[17] However, references to specific female beliefs and customs are obscure in the French records, since the practices the Jesuits recorded were usually the hunting rites of men. But Le Jeune and others did note that women had some special foods, such as the hearts of certain birds, held separate feasts, and performed dances quite different from those of men. In 1691, Le Clercq described a women's dance among the Micmac, an Algonquian-speaking people in the area of the Gulf of St. Lawrence, the Maritime Provinces, and the Gaspé Peninsula, whose belief systems and rituals had many similarities to those of the northern and western hunter-gatherers discussed here: "They draw back and push out the arms, the hands, and the whole body, in a manner altogether hideous, looking intently on the earth as if they would draw out something therefrom by the very strength and force of their contortions."[18] Although women, like men, had supernatural "helpers," Le Jeune also learned that women had a special, innate spiritual potency, strongest during menses and childbirth.[19]

The separate rituals and attributes of the sexes indicate that male and female had distinct gender identities in traditional ideology. This system recognized the autonomy of men and women by emphasizing their different needs and concerns. The division was not disruptive, however, countered as it was by the complementarity of social and productive activities. Instead, the different aspects of female and male combined in a vital symmetry upon which the community's survival depended.

Interaction with Europeans through missions and trade disrupted this balance, for colonization involved more than simply moving people, institutions, and laws to new terrain. While missions and trading posts were not merely transplanted French institutions (in the literal meaning of the term "colonization"), missionaries and traders did expect to change the lives of the natives; it was inherent in the very concept of a "New France" that Indians would eventually conform to the ideological and socioeconomic values of the newcomers. Although some scholars have suggested that the early missionaries presented no real threat to groups such as the Ojibwa, European concepts of social relations, combined with religious and economic programs to colonize New France, slowly undermined the equilibrium of many native communities.[20] The hierarchical social structure and religious values of the French clashed

with the balanced and more harmonious relations of Indian
women and men, altering their productive and spiritual responsibilities.[21]

In evaluating gender-based responses to colonization it is essential that we consider the symbiotic association of religion
and economics in New France. Missionaries did not face virgin
country when they set out to evangelize the *sauvages*. A fundamental economic transformation already had begun as market-
oriented trapping gradually replaced subsistence hunting-
gathering. This shift preceded the mission effort, and paved
the way for it.[22] The fur trade acted as a catalyst for modifications in social and economic structures throughout native
bands, which the Jesuit program of Christianization complemented. During the seventeenth century, the proximity of domiciled Indians to merchants at missions such as Tadoussac,
Trois Rivières, Quebec, and Montréal facilitated their accommodation to French economic practices. Settled Indians and
those groups that kept close seasonal trading contact with the
French experienced gradual changes in both the nature and
significance of their productive activities as their interaction
with European priests and traders became more complex.

Although trade for favored items existed prior to contact
with the French, the concept of undertaking intensive production in order to accumulate and then exchange surplus goods
appears to have been introduced with the fur trade in the sixteenth century. As Nicolas Denys explained:

> The hunting by the Indians in old times was easy for them. They
> killed animals only in proportion as they had need of them. When
> they were tired of eating one sort, they killed some of another. If
> they did not wish longer to eat meat, they caught some fish. They
> never made an accumulation of skins of Moose, Beaver, Otter, or
> others, but only so far as they needed them for personal use.[23]

Early Europeans in New France were dismayed to find that
native peoples placed little value on tangible wealth as a source
of status. Their economic system was more communal than
competitive; each person gained prestige through contributions to the group's welfare. Originally, Indians were hard put
to understand the Europeans' desire for wealth. "You [the

French] are covetous," they reprimanded one missionary, "and are neither generous nor kind; as for us, if we have a morsel of bread we share it with our neighbor."[24] The Montagnais suspected that the French valued material possessions more than native goodwill. Le Jeune recounted with some frustration that "when you refuse anything to a Savage, he immediately says *Khisakhitan*, 'thou lovest that,' *sakhita, sakhita,* 'Love it, love it;' as if they would say that we are attached to what we love, and that we prefer it to their friendship."[25]

This careless attitude toward property would change, the French hoped, once they had enticed the Indians to settle, "for anyone who has taken the trouble to cultivate a piece of land does not readily abandon it, but struggles valiantly to keep it."[26] The French saw a direct relationship between native economic concerns and their own missionary work. They were, in fact, much freer with material aid to those who expressed an interest in conversion. In 1639, the Company of New France, whose shareholders were motivated by religious and national concerns as well as profit, granted settled Christian Indians privileges in their store equal to those of the French. They also offered cleared plots of land as a special inducement to women to convert and marry.[27] Their success in influencing material values was at first limited, however, only to those who had chosen to become Christians and settle. In 1703, Baron Lahontan noted that among the Ojibwa, at least, "money is in use with none of them but those that are Christians, who live in the Suburbs of our Towns."[28]

The interdependent, complementary roles of male and female in sustaining the community began to alter with the introduction of the European-based system of trade.[29] French traders wanted the furs obtained by men rather than the small game, tools, utensils, or clothing procured or produced by women. "They deal principally in Beavers," the Jesuit Charles Lalemant observed in 1626, "in which they find their greatest profit."[30] For groups that participated directly in trade, fur hunting and trapping gradually became the major activity of most men. Because furs served as the medium of exchange for goods, daily and seasonal life for all came increasingly to revolve around the trade. Most of the items given in exchange by

the French were tools and weapons intended to facilitate trapping—which occurred at the expense of subsistence hunting.
Discussing changes in Micmac hunting patterns, Denys explained that the cost of operating muskets made men reluctant
to use ammunition on game not suitable for trade: "It is not
that the choice of small game is not good and abundant there,
but this does not suffice their support, besides which it costs
them too much in powder and ball." To make the focus on fur-
bearers feasible, traders deliberately included foodstuffs in
trade exchanges.[31]

The introduction of and growing dependence on European
goods obtainable primarily with furs not only reoriented male
hunting patterns, but it altered or eliminated many female productive activities as well. Two lists of trade goods exemplify this
change. In his *Relation* of 1616, Biard remarked on the nature
of the trading that took place along the St. Lawrence during
the summer. Indians, he wrote, exchanged skins for "bread,
peas, beans, prunes, tobacco, etc.; kettles, hatchets, iron arrow-
points, awls, puncheons, cloaks, blankets, and all other such
commodities as the French bring them."[32] Ten years later
Lalemant carefully recorded "the merchandise which these
Gentlemen use in trading with the Savages; that is to say the
cloaks, blankets, nightcaps, hats, shirts, sheets, hatchets, iron
arrowheads, bodkins, swords, picks to break the ice in Winter,
knives, kettles, prunes, raisins, Indian corn, peas, crackers or
sea biscuits, and tobacco."[33] These lists suggest that for domiciled Indians and those in the trade, subsistence patterns were
beginning to change dramatically. European merchandise replaced items whose manufacture had previously constituted
some of women's most important productive activities. Where
women had been responsible for processing skins and trans-
forming them into garments, hunters now obtained clothing
with furs. "Now that they trade with the French for capes, blankets, cloths, and shirts," Le Jeune reported, "there are many
who use them."[34] And Biard commented of the Micmac that
"they are also quite willing to make use of our hats, shoes, caps,
woolens and shirts and of our linen."[35]

Although native people did not, of course, immediately buy
all of their clothing from the French, ready-made goods may

have seemed a convenient substitute for time-consuming manufacture of native dress. Acquiring such items from traders also
allowed women to spend more time readying furs for market.
Thus, as women's relationship to the disposal of hides and
furs changed, the significance of their direct contribution to
the community welfare diminished.[36] As for men, while they
too experienced a degree of alienation from the fruit of their
labor, their contribution now became the focal one within the
economy.

The orientation of many female tasks began to shift from the
creation of a useful end product, such as clothing or tools, to
assistance in the preparation of furs. Awls and bodkins that
otherwise might have been used for sewing coats or breechclouts instead enabled a woman to stretch more furs and stretch
them faster. Women were undeniably vital to the production of
the furs that Europeans sought so eagerly—their scraping,
stretching, and tanning of skins was essential to the process. No
longer, however, did they participate as producers in their own
right; rather, they were becoming auxiliaries to the trapping
process.[37]

In groups that had not become sedentary, other items introduced by the French fostered change by allowing greater mobility and flexibility in the search for furs. The copper kettle,
for example, among Micmac at least and one suspects else-
where, replaced the stationary wooden cooking troughs that
had marked frequently used campsites. With the easily port-
able kettle, moves were soon regulated less by custom than by
the desire to increase the fur take.[38] Although access to game
had always been a priority of seasonal nomadism, the new focus
on furs shifted responsibility for moves largely out of women's
control. This was a significant departure from the system in
which "the choice of plans, of undertakings, of journeys, of
winterings, lies in nearly every instance in the hands of the
housewife."[39] Generally, moreover, frequent moves to unfamiliar areas must have been disruptive for women, who were responsible for setting up and tearing down the camp and for
gathering fuel at each new site.[40]

Increased dependence on European foodstuffs affected native women's activities as well. Their food procuring—fishing,

hunting small game, and gathering—was crucial to the aboriginal economy. After the introduction of European food items, however, although women continued to gather nuts and berries when available and to fish, the importance of these subsistence foods decreased as French foods became more accessible. When Le Jeune listed the foods that had been a routine part of the diet of the Montagnais band he wintered with in 1633–34, he included in his notes that "they get from our French People galette, or sea biscuit, bread, prunes, peas, roots, figs, and the like."[41] Women's direct contribution to communal and family well-being diminished as dried peas, bread, and biscuits became common fare acquired by the trapper in exchange for his furs. While certainly the use of European dry staples could provide a buffer between harsh winters and starvation, one suspects that it also eroded the authority that had accompanied women's role in allocating and preparing meat.[42]

This is not to say that women made a rapid shift from being producers to mere processors, or that Indian men ruthlessly exploited women for personal gain. Rather, the fur trade initiated changes in the subsistence activities of women and men, changes that imparted greater economic importance to male labor because European traders hungered for furs. The uneven transmission of European technology to men and women compounded this situation. Muskets and steel traps traded to men in exchange for furs increased their efficiency and potential yield. The items that women received, in contrast, tended to be trinkets or goods such as awls or copper pots, which, while making some tasks easier, were geared toward assisting them in their secondary position as fur processors.[43] In response to French demands, an inequality in the productive values of the sexes had developed that Indians were forced to accept, at least in part, if they were to participate in the fur trade.

The immediate benefits of tools and trade goods probably obscured the economic and technological developments that created this imbalance; moreover, the gradual nature of these changes made it improbable that Indians could respond directly to many of them. But one dimension of the transformations was clearly visible to Indians and could be reckoned with: namely, the clear intent of the missionaries to change rituals and social organization. In particular, Jesuit attempts to form Christian communities provided an immediate focus for the reactions of native men and women to the changes affecting them.

The missionaries labored energetically to effect the spiritual colonization of New France; they were educated and earnest men who worked tirelessly to spread the gospel and promote European cultural values in native communities. The disparities between their worldview and that of their prospective converts, therefore, were an ongoing source of discomfort and irritation. Father Jean de Brebeuf, of the Huron mission of Ste. Marie, wrote to Le Jeune in 1637 with suggestions for instructing new missionaries and explained the problems of life in the field: "Leaving a highly civilized community, you fall into the hands of barbarous people who care but little for your Philosophy or your Theology. All the fine qualities which might make you loved and respected in France are like pearls trampled under the feet of swine, or rather of mules, which utterly despise you when they see that you are not as good pack animals as they are."[44] The Indians, in turn—male and female alike— were often puzzled by the urgency with which priests attempted to change native customs and beliefs. Pierre Biard, of the first Jesuit mission of 1611–16, found that when he argued with natives about some practice, they responded: "That is the Savage way of doing it. You can have your way and we will have ours; every one values his own wares."[45]

The key to inculcating French Christian values, the priests decided, was to encourage Indians to establish permanent settlements near missions and trading centers. "One of the most efficient means we can use to bring them to JESUS CHRIST," Le Jeune suggested in 1638, "is to organize them into a sort of Village."[46] But the seasonal nomadism of the Montagnais did not harmonize well with the collective rituals at the heart of seventeenth-century Catholicism. Nor did native social organization lend itself to the hierarchical system of male secular authority that characterized European society. The Jesuits hoped that offers of material goods might win souls, for "not one of them hopes to be lodged and assisted who does not resolve to be an honest man, and to become a Christian,—so much so

that it is the same thing in a Savage to wish to become sedentary, and to wish to believe in God."[47] Once the natives were
settled, the priests assumed, it would be a simple thing to instruct them in religious devotion and the basics of the Christian
marriage and family. The combined effects of epidemics and
ongoing conflict with Iroquois, coincidentally, aided the Jesuits
in their efforts to establish villages near the missions.

Conversion efforts in these model settlements, however, did
not go as planned. The elderly of both sexes often rejected the
missionaries' evangelizing—though the priests blamed this on
the obstinacy of old age. It was all that could be expected of the
old men, Le Jeune caustically remarked, "whose brains, dried
up in their old maxims, had no longer any fluid in which to receive the impression of our doctrine."[48] Occasionally, whole
bands resisted the Jesuits' advances; as one weary missionary
related, "they even prevented us from entering their villages,
threatening to kill and eat us."[49] But gender differences in responses disturbed the priests even more.

At first the Jesuits focused their proselytizing on men and
boys, alternating attacks on male hunting and divination rituals with blandishments of the comforts and virtue of life as a
Christian man. Modesty and convenience limited their contact
with women. In keeping with Jesuit practice, Le Jeune decided
that "in regard to the women, it is not becoming for us to receive them into our houses," and effectively barred them from
participation in most religious instruction.[50] But then, the
priests expected women to convert as a matter of course, if only
because the "neophytes" needed Christian wives to minimize
the temptation of backsliding. Christian men who married pagan girls, Le Jeune feared, would, "as their husbands, be compelled to follow them and thus fall back onto barbarism or to
leave them, another evil full of danger."[51] So although the Jesuits needed female converts to meet the goal of establishing
sedentary villages based on the nuclear family structure, they
initially planned to leave the instruction of women to chance or
to male converts.[52]

Some women did accept the Jesuits' teachings. In fact, the
speed with which several Attikamek women attained baptismal
status confounded Jérôme Lalemant, who had assumed that

their emotional tendencies would preclude any interest in religion. "What seems quite astonishing is," he reported, "that the women are in no respect behind the men in the performance of that duty. As they are naturally affectionate and more pressing, they have less of worldly respect in connection with these strange things, which are so holy and so useful to these people, who have remained for so many centuries in the shadows of death."[53] Paul Rageuneau also found some female converts very concerned about how to structure their relationships with God, noting in particular one woman who staunchly maintained her Christian faith despite persecution from others in her small band. Even the gloomy Father André at Green Bay reported with surprise in 1674 that "several women were very assiduous in their attendance, a thing I had not yet observed."[54]

Others, such as the young woman whom Le Jeune had consigned to the dungeon, clearly opted for conversion over flogging or imprisonment—an understandable choice.[55] In certain instances, too, baptism may have decreased French pressures on a community and alleviated tensions that arose, for example in the village of St. Joseph, from conflict over religious allegiances. And at least superficial observance of Christian practices perhaps enabled women to divert the missionaries' attention from themselves.[56]

If they converted, women tended to interpret and manipulate Christianity to serve their own needs.[57] Indeed, Catholic mysticism proved a useful tool in their continued emphasis of the sexual distinctions and female autonomy that had distinguished precolonial society. In 1691, Le Clercq, describing the activities of certain Micmac converts who emulated the missionaries, was surprised by the number of women involved. Moreover, he worried about their increased authority in the community:

> These, in usurping the quality and the name of *religieuses*, say certain prayers in their own fashion, and affect a manner of living more reserved than that of the commonalty of Indians, who allow themselves to be dazzled by the glamour of a false and ridiculous devotion. They look upon these women as extraordinary persons, whom they believe to hold converse, to speak familiarly, and to

hold communication with the sun, which they have all adored as their divinity.[58]

By the 1670s a virtual cult of the Virgin had developed in some mission communities as women converts focused their ritual attention on that consummate symbol of femaleness in Catholic ideology. Ursuline convents—the ultimate separate institution for females within the church—became gathering places for Christian women. There they continued to stress older values of female autonomy, but now in a format acceptable to the demands of the missionaries.[59]

More frequently, however, to the missionaries' dismay, women declined conversion and instead stressed the importance of older rituals and practices. Women scorned priests and converts alike for flouting tradition, and they had little patience for Christians who threatened eternal damnation to those who clung to heathen practices. The confrontation between the men and women of St. Joseph's at Sillery clearly was not an isolated incident. Indeed, the Jesuits recorded similar episodes throughout New France, for the missionary effort soon proved a divisive force in many native communities, with women and men reacting differently to Jesuit proselytizing. In villages with Jesuit missionaries, the opinions expressed by women differed sharply from those of men. The Jesuits, Lahontan reported, had insisted that "a Fire is Kindled in the other World to Torment 'em for ever, unless they take more care to correct Vice. To such Remonstrances the Men reply, 'That's Admirable;' and the Women usually tell the Good Fathers in a deriding way, 'That if their Threats be well grounded, the Mountains of the other World must consist of the Ashes of souls.' "[60]

Le Jeune recounted in 1640 that the wife of one convert from Sagné, "a rough and wild creature, who gives a great deal of trouble to the poor man," refused to consider conversion when "Charles" insisted that he must have a Christian wife. The priest described the man's anxiety over the situation: " 'You have told me that those who do evil are very often incited to it by Demons; alas!' said he, 'then I am always with some Demon, for my wife is always angry; I fear that the Demons she keeps in my cabin are perverting the good that I received in holy Baptism.' " The fellow confided that she had hurled a knife at him during an argument over her refusal to convert. The woman spurned his efforts—he even had volunteered to do her chores if she converted—and mocked his faith. " 'Dost thou not see that we are all dying since they told us to pray to God?' " she asked, as would many others throughout New France. " 'Where are thy relatives? Where are mine? the most of them are dead; it is no longer a time to believe.' "[61]

Other male converts had equal difficulty convincing wives to become Christians and grew increasingly aggressive and punitive in their attempts to secure a conversion. Le Jeune found the male converts' zeal gratifying; he observed that "there was nothing that they would not do or endure in order to secure obedience to God."[62] Women's husbands and brothers beat them in punishment for defiance, sometimes with the full support of the missionaries, who believed that the Indians were finally learning the importance of exercising justice.[63] The zealous Christian relatives of one unconverted young woman flogged her publicly for not discouraging an unconverted suitor; they forced the other girls in the community to watch the display and warned them that similar punishment awaited further rebellion.[64]

While these incidents may not have been daily occurrences, the conflict between females who retained customary beliefs and male converts and priests was an ongoing one with little evident potential for resolution. No one was "more attached to these silly customs [here, vision quests], or more obstinate in clinging to this error, than the old women, who will not even lend an ear to our instructions," wrote Father Dablon from the Ottawa mission of Sault Ste. Marie in 1669. He cited as example an incident following the conversion of four young sisters, when "an old woman who was strongly attached to her superstitions, rudely scolded them,—telling them, among other things, that Baptism was invented only to cause death, and that they must fully expect to die soon."[65]

Father Louis André at Green Bay found the women there equally resistant. When his cabin mysteriously burned in 1672, André was certain they had put it to the torch, for "the old women especially blamed me greatly because I said that The evil spirit should be neither obeyed nor feared."[66] Although he eventually convinced some women to convert, André never really trusted them. It seemed to him that women were too steeped in paganism from birth. Their real objection to Christianity, he decided, was that it involved more work than they were accustomed to. Describing the vision fast undergone by adolescents, he, like Dablon, insisted that "the women are the Cause of this evil practice, even more than The men; For—in order to save themselves The trouble of preparing Food, or to economize their provisions, or to accustom Their children to eat only at night—they make Them fast like Dogs."[67] André's caustic observations were not altogether wrong in positing a relationship between women's emphasis on tradition and the more prosaic aspects of daily life. The women's refusal to convert was certainly a protest, but not simply of an increased work load. They may well have been responding to the redefinition of female and male identities and status.

The Jesuits' efforts to instill Christianity came in the wake of the fur trade and capitalized on the vulnerability of Indian communities weakened by imported epidemic diseases and the extermination of peltry animals through overhunting.[68] By introducing alien cultural values into groups already exhausted by inexplicable changes and newly settled near missions or trading centers, the missionaries actively helped to alter traditional gender relationships.

The system of balanced yet autonomous male and female roles baffled, even horrified, the priests. To cope, they automatically assigned each sex a place within the Western scheme of gender relations. Therefore, in observing women's camp-oriented activities, they assumed that the sexual division of labor reflected status, as it did in Europe: women's food processing, tool making, and camp tasks were manual work and thus drudgery. Noting that men hunted large game—an activity reserved for the privileged in Europe—whereas women generally remained near the camp, one early missionary concluded in 1610 that Micmac women's "duties and positions are those of slaves, laborers and beasts of burden"—hardly the most tempting targets for a conversion effort.[69]

The priests' confrontation with native women as autonomous, sexually active females provided yet another opportunity for misunderstanding. Monogamous, permanent marriage based on masculine authority and the control of women's activities and sexuality characterized French social organization and was integral to the system that the Jesuits struggled to establish in New France.[70] They found, however, that prospective converts did not share their views on authority, marriage, or sex. Indian women's power in the family and community shocked them. As Le Clercq explained in 1691, "The men leave the arrangements of the housekeeping to the women, and do not interfere with them. . . . I can say that I have never seen the head of the wigwam where I was living ask of his wife what had become of the meat of moose and of beaver."[71]

Le Jeune described more exactly what disturbed him about native marriage when he related an incident in which he tried to persuade a headman to enroll his son in mission school. When the man deferred to his wife's wish that the child remain at home, the priest complained that "the women have great power here. A man may promise you something, and, if he does not keep his promise, he thinks he is sufficiently excused when he tells you that his wife did not wish to do it. I told him then that he was the master, and that in France women do not rule their husbands."[72] By the good father's standards, gender relations in New France were definitely askew. He and others therefore encouraged male converts to assert their wills and exact obedience from recalcitrant spouses.[73]

But the unsettling aspects of Indians' marital relations paled when viewed against their amorous affairs, for women and men controlled their own pre- and postmarital sexual activities. While most missionaries and travelers agreed that the Micmac generally were monogamous and favored premarital chastity, on the whole native sexual mores appalled them. A description sent by Father Allouez in 1667 from the Ottawa mission conveyed his horror:

> The fountain-head of their Religion is libertinism; and all these various sacrifices end ordinarily in debauches, indecent dances, and shameful acts of concubinage. All the devotion of the men is

directed toward securing many wives, and changing them whenever they choose; that of the women, toward leaving their husbands; and that of the girls, toward a life of profligacy.[74]

The priests found the ease with which native couples di-
vorced equally outrageous. "The stability of marriage is one of
the most perplexing questions in the conversion and settlement
of the Savages," wrote Le Jeune's successor, Vimont, in 1642;
"we have much difficulty in obtaining and in maintaining it."[75]
And Pierre Boucher, a governor of Trois Rivières and resident
of New France from 1635 to 1717, observed that "divorce is not
an odious thing among them Indians. . . . For when a woman
wishes to put away her husband, she has only to tell him to
leave the house, and he goes out of it without another word."[76]
In fact, most native peoples found divorce quite acceptable if a
couple had a hostile or unsatisfying relationship. Women felt
free to leave spouses who were poor or lazy hunters or otherwise were inadequate as mates.[77]

The Jesuits found this situation untenable and realized that
sexual freedom, divorce, and polygamy had to be eliminated if
native Christian communities were to be established. By 1638,
they had decided that dispensing land and money might be the
most tempting inducement to marital fidelity, "for a husband
will not so readily leave a wife who brings him a respectable
dowry; and a woman, having her possessions near our French
settlements, will not readily leave them, any more than her
husband"—or so they hoped.[78] The missionaries, convinced
that "it was not honorable for a woman to love anyone else
except her husband," worked hard to get women to accept
monogamy.[79] But they often had to rely on male converts to
enforce observation of this alien practice. In one notable instance, zealous Christians at Sillery captured a woman who had
left her husband and imprisoned her without food, fire, or
cover in early January of 1642.[80]

Women, particularly non-Christians, resisted the change because it was not to their advantage. Although they undoubtedly
wanted to retain control over their sexual activities, they also
objected to monogamy for more practical reasons, such as its
impact on the system of sororal polygyny, in which sisters could

be married to the same man. The practice was found in many groups. For example, Charles Albanel reported sororal polygyny among Mistassini Cree, usually following the death of a sister's spouse. A Montagnais convert told Le Jeune in 1637 that "since I have been preaching among them that a man should have only one wife I have not been well received by the women; for, since they are more numerous than the men, if a man can only marry one of them, the others will have to suffer. Therefore this doctrine is not according to their liking."[81] Disease and Iroquois attacks had decimated the population, taking the greatest toll among men; the result, reported Barthelemy Vimont in 1644, was that "these remnants of Nations consist almost entirely of women, widows or girls, who cannot all find lawful husbands."[82] But despite the uneven sex ratio, when men became Christians it was incumbent upon them to become monogamous as well. "Those who had left their first wives are taking them back," Druilletes observed from the Sault mission to the Ottawa in 1671, "while those who had several are keeping only the first and discarding the others."[83] Men's acceptance of Christianity, therefore, removed the possibility of marriage for many women, consigning them to a life of social and economic uncertainty.

Despite its negative impact on women, Christian European culture appears to have attracted men, especially those involved in the fur trade. The fact that priests and traders initially targeted men undoubtedly contributed to their greater receptivity. More significantly, conversion placed the individual in the good graces of the clergy and the French colonial government. Christians thus had a decided advantage in terms of access to French goods and protection.[84] When conversion accompanied settlement in a mission village, a neophyte found himself strategically located near the very source of the fur trade. Proximity to missionaries was a further asset in that it was they who legitimized men's newly elevated position within domiciled groups. The Montagnais and other eastern subarctic and Great Lakes groups traditionally had no institutionalized decision-making process, no distinction of "formal" and "informal" to separate the household from the group. Establishing a definite sociopolitical structure with a recognized "chief" was therefore a major goal of the missionaries.[85] The priests expected men, as members of a European-patterned community, to exercise authority over women, the family, and political affairs. Sedentary life made this new pattern possible by creating nuclear families, which functioned independently of one another, out of groups that had been largely cooperative.[86]

The transition from subsistence hunter to fur trapper demanded another social accommodation by men, which the move to the *reserve* made easier. The communal relations vital to a group's survival in the bush were not really appropriate to a market-oriented economy centered on trapping, where individual accumulation of furs for trade, not the group's welfare, was the important goal. By 1642, Christian men from the settlements had begun to avoid hunting with the "pagans," preferring to go alone or with a few other Christians. Of course, sincere concern for their spiritual integrity may have motivated this change, but it also coincided rather well with the more competitive approach necessary for successful commercial trapping. The emphasis in the mission villages on the nuclear family appears to have decreased traditional pressures for cooperative hunting and food sharing and, in turn, encouraged a greater individualism among the hunters-turned-trappers.[87]

At initial contact, the hunt had been more than a routine productive activity: it was virtually a religious vocation and not easily abandoned, one would suspect, for the more prosaic labor of trapping. Hunting had provided the very foundation of a man's social and religious identity. Perhaps spiritual crisis was the culminating factor in a man's decision to convert; certainly economic and status motivation alone cannot account for the shift from traditional hunter to Christian trapper. It is provocative that Christianity apparently appealed most to men who no longer identified themselves primarily as hunters. Indeed, throughout the *Relations* the Jesuits observe that men accuse the old religion of not working for them; they had, they said, lost touch with the supernaturals and animal guardians on whom they depended.[88] Shamans, the intermediaries between the natural and supernatural realms, "now universally complain that their Devils have lost much of their power, if compared with what it is said to have been in the time of their

Ancestors," Biard recorded as early as 1614.[89] Ironically, the intensely personal nature of a hunter's or shaman's liaison with his "helpers" may have smoothed the way for conversion. The individualism of a Christian's relationship with his God must have seemed similar to the one-on-one association developed with supernaturals. Alienated from their traditional source of self-definition by forces they could no longer rationalize, men appear to have found in Christianity a reasonable substitute.[90]

Women, however, were generally more reluctant to accept either the new religion or its followers. They apparently perceived little advantage in Christianity, finding instead that it imposed unfamiliar and unwelcome limitations on them. The reciprocity and interdependence that had previously governed the relationships between men and women were missing from the *reserves*, where missionaries worked to establish a hierarchy of stratified gender roles and status—a reflection of their own class-bound understanding of French social order. Priests and colonial officials deliberately and persistently stressed the importance of male authority in the community and family and of women's obligation to obedience. The settled life and nuclear family pattern advocated by the Jesuits to civilize the Indians encouraged the breakdown of the flexible, multifamily units based, apparently, on matrilocal principles, thus further weakening women's position in the community.[91] When male converts accepted this system and acted accordingly, women stood to lose both status and self-determination.

Another factor in women's poor reception of Christianity may have been that their personal spiritual development did not depend solely on individual rapport with supernaturals. Although the failure of the shamans' power undoubtedly disturbed women, they were not as susceptible to the disruption of relationships with "helpers" as men were. Their primary source of spiritual strength was largely internal, and so less vulnerable; because they probably did not experience the erosion of belief to the degree that many hunters did, they had little need for the replacement offered by Christianity.

Moreover, while Christianity's emphasis on individualism attracted men, it may have alienated women. Their social orientation had been more communal than that of men: they performed many of their activities in groups and collectively controlled the camp area. One can speculate that the Jesuits, in their efforts to establish Christian nuclear families, were well aware that by isolating women from one another and decreasing their cooperative and ritual activities they undermined the community of women who opposed them. While the groups considered in this chapter were unique because of their domiciled status, their situation nevertheless offers a portent of changes that gradually occurred among other Indians in New France. Their experiences were, in effect, a trial run in the colonizing ventures that soon engulfed native peoples throughout the interior of Canada and the Upper Great Lakes.

2

BETWEEN THE MISSIONARY ERAS

The antagonism between women and men that characterized many domiciled bands and others within the Jesuits' scope did not wash across the boreal forests in the ensuing years. But the record does suggest that in the priests' wake an undercurrent of disagreement—centering on loyalty to traditional ways—gradually caused a pattern of gender-based tensions. This was a slow process, however, which affected groups unevenly and manifested itself only subtly.

Jesuit efforts among Cree, Ojibwa, and Montagnais-Naskapi proceeded fitfully throughout the late seventeenth and early eighteenth centuries. Competition with other religious orders and the establishment of a diocesan organization in 1658 hampered the missionaries' freedom of movement. Traders and government officials, moreover, aggravated by the priests' long-standing opposition to the practice of plying Indians with brandy during fur trading sessions, generally did little to bolster the Jesuits' activities.[1] Intertribal warfare also took its toll on the missions. In 1670, the Tadoussac Montagnais escaped the ravages of Iroquois raids and smallpox epidemics by fleeing north to James Bay, and by 1685 the Jesuits had abandoned the mission at Sillery to the military following similar Montagnais dispersals. Although Father François de Crespieul tried to maintain a steady field presence among the Montagnais from 1660 until his death in 1703, the mission languished until rebuilt by Father Pierre Lauré in the 1720s. Finally, many Indians had become disenchanted with the Jesuits, whose novelty had worn thin. The priests were hard taxed in some areas to retain the loyalty and buttress the faith of converted Indians.[2]

The northern Great Lakes missions had their problems as well. With the death of Father Charles Albanel in 1696, the mission at Sault Ste. Marie collapsed; the crown order of 1697 that closed the fur trade led to the abandonment of the posts at St. Ignace (Fort Buade) and Michilimackinac (Mackinac).[3] By 1711, bereft of converts, the Jesuits had relinquished Mackinac. Although they revived the mission in 1715, when the French reopened the military and trading posts, it now served an exclusively French and métis (mixed-blood) congregation. Their Indian activities increasingly revolved around the Huron and Iroquois missions along the St. Lawrence and among Illinois tribes to the south.[4]

The Jesuits' domain continued to dwindle as the crown pressured the troublesome order and finally restricted it in 1761, effectively blocking recruitment to the remaining New France missions. Control of the territory passed to the British through the Treaty of Paris two years later; thus, when Pope Clement XIV suppressed the Society of Jesus worldwide in 1773, Britain dissolved the order and claimed the Jesuits' Canadian holdings. The missionaries, their numbers now reduced by death to eleven, fought the edict for sixteen years, but as the priests expired so did their posts. Tadoussac fell in 1782, and by the end of that year only four fatigued and elderly Jesuits survived. They dropped all pretense of missionary work to concentrate on protecting their holdings from the Protestants, relinquishing the establishments only in 1790, when the British guaranteed to convert the Indians. The Jesuit missions had come full circle; the remaining clerics completed their days as pensioners, performing charitable deeds until the last died in 1800.[5]

The declining years of the Jesuit missions resulted in a hiatus in missionary activity in the interior; for a span of eighty years Ojibwa, Cree, and Montagnais-Naskapi rarely encountered missionaries. Throughout the eighteenth century most North American colonial denominations neglected Indian missions to focus on their own growth, while European missionary societies ceased most activities following the American Revolution.[6] Christianity's prospects among the native populations thus hinged on the influence of converts and the tenacity of traditionalists in each band, as heightened mobility during this period removed Indians further from the missions spiritually, temporally, and geographically.

Native territories shifted from the 1660s on as the fur trade sparked Ojibwa expansion west and northwest from Lake Superior. Displaced bands of Cree, having retreated into the hinterland beyond Lake Winnipeg, were frequently compelled to trade through Ojibwa and Ottawa go-betweens. But when the Hudson's Bay Company secured posts on western James Bay and Hudson Bay after 1670, virtually all groups between the bays and Lake Superior gravitated toward the British commerce. Impressive contingents of up to fifteen hundred Inland Cree trekked to York Factory on Hudson Bay for the spring trading. Spurred to compete, the French created the Compagnie du Nord in 1676 and opened for business at Fort Camanistogoyan on Thunder Bay, Fort la Maune on Lake Nipigon, and Fort de Français (in 1685) on the Albany River. By the 1730s, French posts festooned the forests west and northwest of Lake Superior, setting off yet another movement of Ojibwa and Cree—this time westward—which lasted four decades.[7]

Montagnais and Naskapi on the lower Labrador Peninsula and Eastern Cree at James Bay also increased their mobility. During the sixteenth and most of the seventeenth centuries the French had encouraged them to bring pelts down to the St. Lawrence. By the late 1600s, as the British established trading posts on the eastern coasts of Hudson and James bays, the Montagnais, Naskapi, and Cree moved into the north and to the eastern bush of Labrador. Contact with Europeans steadily decreased, to the point that James McKenzie, admittedly an unsympathetic observer, reported that the Naskapi were practically in an aboriginal state. "The Nascapees may still be regarded as the primitive inhabitants of the coast," he explained,

whose ancient habits, usages and absurdities they, to this day, retain in all their savage purity. . . . They resort with their bear, marten, fox, and carribou skins once a year, either to Hudson's Bay, Great Esquimaux Bay, or the King's Post, to exchange them for the most necessary articles, such as axes, knives, guns, ammunition, &c. Their number is about five hundred souls, and there are some among them who have grown old without having ever seen an European, and who still form their utensils out of bones and stones.[8]

The bounding competition between eighteenth-century English and French fur traders incited economic and political disorder, provoking further turmoil in native communities. Although the Compagnie du Nord vied mightily with the Hudson's Bay Company (HBC), its competitive edge had flagged by midcentury. Then, in the 1760s, an influx of French-Canadian and Scots traders from Montréal revitalized the rivalry, and the HBC, finding itself on the defensive, was forced to construct new posts farther inland. With the establishment of the early North West Company in 1779 by a syndicate of fur-trading firms, the fur trade verged on open conflict. The HBC again increased its territory and forts, with trading posts now following aggressive factors who struggled to stake their turf in the interior forests. For Indians, these developments provided a fine opportunity to play the contending traders against one another and obtain the best credit for furs. HBC factors, North West Company traders, and agents of the short-lived X.Y. Company (1798–1804) found themselves unhappily courting Indian trade.[9] "The consequence will be," one trader groused, "that the Indians will get all they want for half the value and laugh at them all, in the end. . . . The Indians have lost all industry and are becoming careless about hunting and paying their credits, as they very well know that no one will refuse."[10]

But the coalition of the HBC and the North West Company in 1821, together with ecological changes, conspired to deprive Indians of the upper hand. By 1805, unchecked beaver trapping had diminished the pelt harvest, affecting much of the northern interior within the decade and forcing Indians to turn to smaller peltry animals such as marten and muskrat. The virtual elimination of moose and caribou populations during this period also removed a mainstay of Cree and Ojibwa subsistence, making starvation a frequent specter. The situation created by the merger of the Hudson's Bay and North West companies, which led to new policies on debts and summer furs and the closing of several posts, proved disastrous. Indians found credit cut, prices up, access to trade goods severely curtailed, and furs rejected. With the shortage of "country" food, they became increasingly dependent on the trading posts for foodstuffs during harsh winters.[11] Many found themselves bound to the Europeans, restricted to the vicinity of the posts by their reliance on trade goods.

Reduced mobility and the emphasis on fishing and hunting small game also resulted in relatively stable hunting groups based in villages near important lakes and rivers. In addition, native men gradually took over fishing and the snaring of small animals, activities that before the 1820s had generally been women's responsibility. In earlier years, "any young man would think himself disgraced [to] even be seen setting a Net to catch fish or a Snare for Rabbit," Charles McKenzie had reported, "& when recourse was had to such means in the times of scarcity it was left entirely to the women's province."[12] Because hares and martens were the women's own property, snaring had provided them with collateral for trading and bargaining. By the 1830s, however, younger men had taken over many of these activities—and simultaneously, fish and hare became more crucial to the diet. This shift had significant economic implications, which were later compounded when fishing became the primary source of cash.[13]

Throughout the chaotic period in which these changes transpired, traders, factors, and explorers pursued their fortunes and curiosity into the interior, seeking native contacts for furs and building new posts. While the overt goal was profit, personal religious commitment often aroused in these men a keen interest in native spirituality, and in journals, diaries, and reports they frequently expounded on the inner life of Indian communities.[14] To be sure, the Europeans' particular purposes in being in this land shaped their narrative depictions of what they encountered; nevertheless, their records provide an occasional glimpse of gender relations among native groups in this period of limited missionary activity but momentous socioeconomic change.

Traders and explorers generally shared the Jesuits' conviction that native women were debased, especially among Western and Plains Cree beyond Lake Superior.[15] Henry Kelsey, a Hudson's Bay Company trader from 1687 to 1724, insisted that Western Cree men considered a woman merely "a Slead dog or Bitch."[16] Although Peter Grant, a trader at Lac la Pluie, concurred that women were drudges and slaves, in his 1804 treatise on the Saulteux he wrote that Ojibwa women were nonetheless a force to be reckoned with: "They are not . . . without their Xanthippes, who, equal to the most celebrated heroines of the ancients and moderns, can assert the rights of their sex, with a vengeance."[17] Philip Turnor and other HBC factors found, on journeys from York Fort to Cumberland House in 1778–79, that they needed a solid reserve of trinkets if they were to compete successfully with Canadian traders. "Such like presents greatly gain the Love of the Women," Turnor observed with exasperation, "and some of them have great influence over their Husbands particularly the Young people who would carry part of their Furrs to the Canadians if it was for those trinkets only."[18] John McDonnell, a North West Company trader at Red River, similarly concluded in 1797 that among the Cree at River la Souris, "daughters are as much esteemed as sons by the Indians, and, indeed, they bring them much greater emoluments. . . . Women, in general, have a great ascendency over their husbands."[19]

David Thompson, a seasoned veteran of the bush married to a mixed-blood Ojibwa, was one of the most astute observers of native life during the period. Apprenticed to the HBC at the age of fourteen, he worked for first the HBC and then the North West Company from 1784 to 1812. As a young trader, he often was the sole European traveling in company with "packet Indians" who carried messages between the far-flung posts. Their companionship on those trips introduced him to belief systems and lifeways that intrigued him and prompted his intensive study of their cultures. Thompson eventually focused on the Cree from Ile à la Crosse and the Churchill River, whom he considered uniform in their beliefs and "the only Natives that have some remains of ancient times from tradition"— besides, that is, the closely related Ojibwa, "the religionists of the North."[20] As he transcribed tales and gathered information in the course of his journeys, Thompson recorded only practices he believed to be untainted by European influences. He relied exclusively on old men for facts about customs and rituals, deeming younger people unsatisfactory informants at best. Yet even though he depended on elderly men to supply details, his commentary stressed women's emphasis on traditional observances. This fact suggests that he was unable to obtain female informants: women may have been reluctant to associate with him or to provide him information on their practices.[21]

Thompson, like all Europeans, was struck by gender differences in the bands he sojourned with, but the position of women among the Cree, "who think much of their women, and love brave men," particularly impressed him.[22] He was convinced that females were the stauncher traditionalists, and although they took unabashed delight in European baubles and tools, Thompson judged women less susceptible than men to Christian influence. "I found many of the men, especially those who had been much in company with white men, to be all half infidels," he reported, "but the Women kept them in order; for they fear the Manito's [supernatural helpers]."[23]

In his *Narrative*, Thompson recalled an instance when some women wanting beads and ribbons agreed to supply him in exchange with marten skins:

> Early the next morning, five young women set off to make Marten Traps; and did not return until the evening. They were rallied by their husbands and brothers; who proposed they should dance to the Manito of the Martens, to this they willingly consented, it was a fine, calm moonlight night, the young men came with the Rattle and Tambour, about nine women formed the dance, to which they sung with their fine voices, and lively they danced hand in hand in a half circle for a long hour; it is now many years ago, yet I remember this gay hour.[24]

While the men on this occasion obviously encouraged the propitiatory dancing, Thompson felt that overall women expressed far more concern with ritual practices than did younger men. They carefully disposed of animal remains to avoid displeasing the game's spirit and prudently placated the supernaturals who controlled the bush. He noted, moreover, that when villagers gathered around the fires on a winter's evening it was women who awed and intrigued them with tales of the creation and the exploits of trickster heroes—of times when people were stronger, animals more numerous, and humans could converse with the bear and the beaver.[25]

Duncan Cameron, like Thompson, was a veteran of the bush who began his career with the Northwest Company in 1786 and later headed its Nipigon, Lac la Pluie, and Red River districts until being captured by the HBC in 1816.[26] He, too, frequently queried old men about their practices, and his long years in the field provided him ample opportunity to scrutinize Cree and Ojibwa lifeways. Many of the observations in his 1804 commentary and journal focus on gender relations. Women's heavy manual labor disposed him to tag them as social inferiors, "mere slaves to their husbands."[27] He described in wearisome detail their preparation of furs, food, and fires, care of the lodges, and fishing activities. Onerous as some of these chores undoubtedly were, Cameron seemed unaware that the domestic responsibilities of Euro-American women were at least as burdensome, and further complicated by larger families.[28] But he observed that native men certainly were not indolent, and he even gave a nod to the interdependency of many male and female tasks:

> The men hunt, build canoes, (which the women sew and pitch,) snowshoe frames ready to net and which the women must finish; they make axehelves, paddles, *traines* for hauling in winter and every other crooked knife work [carving]. Still, they undergo as great hardships in winter as the women, for very often one man has to hunt and provide for fourteen or fifteen persons.

Although he maintained his conviction that women's position was a lowly one, he did admit that "some of the bolder hussies nevertheless make themselves very independent and 'wear the breeches' when the husband happens to be good natured."[29]

Native women's staunch loyalty to traditional practices amused Cameron, and, while not claiming that religiosity had disappeared among men, he contended that males exploited women's beliefs in order to control their behavior. He gave as an example the sacred, or medicine, bundle that most men carried: "Women are as much afraid to touch it as they would be to touch a venimous snake or toad. These women are very credulous and their husbands make them believe whatever they please and, among other things, that by virtue of this bag they will know whenever their wives prove unfaithful to them or misbehave in anything."[30] Hudson's Bay Company factor James Isham said much the same: "The men pretends to be great Conjurer's, tho' Know nothing of any such artifice, and all I cou'd make of itt, is Very Eronious and purely Design'd to frigh'n the women and Children."[31]

Initially, these seem little more than diverting examples of naive wives gulled by scheming husbands, but on further consideration they suggest that although females and males both continued to refer to traditional beliefs, their reasons for doing so were beginning to diverge. Men, it appears, deliberately used medicine bundles to manipulate their wives, but women may have employed credulity to their own advantage. Their loyalty to the old system allowed them to retain control over their personal activities, as Cameron's account reveals: "The consequence of this [use of the medicine bags] is that they [women] are pretty chaste when sober, but when the least in liquor, they indulge themselves in such sport as comes their way; when found out, they will say they remember nothing about it, and were senseless at the time, so that it was not they who misbehaved but the liquor [the liquor's spirit]."[32] Because Ojibwa, Cree, and other Algonquians believed that liquor—or the bottle in which it came—contained supernatural entities that oversaw their actions, an individual was not responsible for anything he or she did while under the influence. The women, therefore, could blame any misconduct found out by the medicine bundles on the liquor.

This behavior suggests a continuity with the pattern established during the Jesuits' tenure: namely, women continued to adhere to older beliefs and did not hesitate to use tradition to protect themselves against men's efforts to regulate their lives. Cameron's account did not intend to suggest open conflict between the sexes, but he did depict a society in which men—perhaps influenced by stepped-up contact with European culture and values—attempted to establish new controls over women. In response, women gradually developed tactics that, by capitalizing on the leeway that traditional beliefs provided (in this instance, regarding the supernatural powers of liquor), avoided direct confrontation yet allowed them to retain independence. Women's ritual observances worked to their advantage; whether their allegiance was heartfelt or calculated, tradition afforded them a means of retaining control, a strategy for surviving in a rapidly changing world.

The case of Net-no-kwa, a powerful figure in her community, illustrates this point. She was an Ottawa living among Ojibwa north of Mackinac and also foster mother of the captive John Tanner, whom she adopted in the 1780s as a replacement for her own dead son. "I have never met with an Indian, either man or woman," Tanner asserted, "who had so much authority as Net-no-kwa. She could accomplish whatever she pleased, either with the traders or the Indians; probably, in some measure, because she never attempted to do any thing which was not right and just."[33] She reinforced her authority through a pronounced reliance on tradition. Tanner cited, for example, an instance when, at a time when band provisions were perilously low, she dreamed of a fat bear's hiding place. For Ojibwa, Cree, and other Algonquians, dreams were an essential conduit for communication with the supernatural world and a validation of one's spiritual condition. Hunting dreams came to women and men alike. Animal spirits visited individuals when food was scarce, revealing lure songs, prescribing propitiatory rituals, or indicating the location of game.[34] Tanner admired the results of Net-no-kwa's dreaming but believed that his mother had tracked the bear to its lodge in advance. He thought perhaps she feigned spiritual validation when it was not immediately forthcoming: "Artifices of this kind, to make her people believe she had intercourse with the Great Spirit, were, I think, repeatedly assayed by her."[35] Whether Tanner's charge resulted from simple disbelief or actual observation of Net-no-kwa's deception is impossible to determine. Be that as it may, Net-no-kwa's dreams—real or otherwise—did reinforce her prestige in the band. Similarly, Blue Robed Cloud, of Chequamegon Bay, had gained spiritual power from a vision received during her first menstrual seclusion, which she used to assist male hunters in finding game.[36]

Women's involvement in the Midewiwin (Mide), or Medicine Lodge Society, further indicates how they used religion to remain a force in their communities. This society, oriented around curing rites, flourished among the same Ojibwa whose powerful shamans and profuse rituals had so impressed David Thompson.[37] Widespread among Southern Ojibwa, the movement also claimed followers as far north as Berens River in Manitoba and Ontario. Although the Midewiwin may have been a revitalization movement organized in response to European incursions, by the eighteenth and early nineteenth centuries its elements were clearly Ojibwa and consistent with aboriginal concepts of the supernatural, probably derived from shamanistic practices and earlier medicine societies. It also drew loosely allied kin groups together into unified communities as migrating Ojibwa formed new, larger villages at trading sites on Lake Superior.[38]

According to North West Company trader Peter Grant,

> no people are more tenacious in their religious opinions, and less communicative on religious subjects than the Sauteux [Saulteaux Ojibwa]. To question them on such a subject [the Midewiwin] is not only frivolous, in their opinion, but impertinent; some will laugh and pretend ignorance on the subject, others will relate, with a most serious air, a long story of absurdities which they had by tradition from their ancestors.[39]

Mide membership was attainable through participation as a patient in curing rituals, but position as an officer in the society came only after lengthy, expensive instruction (one nineteenth-century initiate paid thirty thousand dollars in beaver pelts)[40] and a formal initiation. The Mide taught herbal knowledge and proper ethical behavior and honoring of manitous to maintain health. "The *Mitewie* is a mysterious ceremony, rather of the nature of our Free Masonry," Grant explained in 1804, "but with this remarkable difference that both sexes are equally admitted as members. Those who put up for candidates must be of a respectable footing in society and make presents to satisfy the number of members requisite to constitute the meeting of the Order."[41]

The Mide stressed traditional beliefs that acknowledged both women's ritual and actual importance in the community. Even into the twentieth century, Midewiwin origin tales emphasized women's centrality: "First a woman was born and then a man was born . . . the woman wondered how she would multiply. So the Great Spirit allowed the woman a man, knowing her wishes. Thus Indians originated."[42] Another version, perhaps an interesting twist on Christian lore, described how the Great Spirit fashioned the first Indian from a handful of dirt:

> At the assembly, the Indian had noticed that the Characters [manitous] were two of a kind, of animal, bird, and fish. And she . . . wondered why she was all by herself—for the first Indian was a woman. All the Characters read her thoughts. The Indian requested that the animal [of Earth] or fowl [of Sky] Spirit make her an Indian companion. A spirit was named to meet this wish. As the woman slept, he moved around her to see if he could detach a part of her body from which to shape another Indian. Finally he removed the woman's lower rib. So on wakening, the woman found herself lying with another person, made like herself. That is why a woman has fewer ribs, on both sides, than a man.[43]

Tanner's mother, Net-no-kwa, was a regular at Mide ceremonies; the Midewiwin undoubtedly provided her and other women with an avenue both for communicating with supernaturals and for enhancing their authority.[44]

The development of the Wabeno, or Wabenowin, one of several rival cults to the Mide, suggests that women needed to protect their interests—religious and otherwise. According to David Thompson, the movement flourished among the culturally alienated, those to whom "it appeared the old Songs, Dances, and Ceremonies by frequent repetition had lost all their charms, and religious attention." He stated that the Wabeno sprang from the dreams of several disaffected chiefs who claimed that all the order's belongings were sacred. By 1798 the movement, which promised hunting success, had been strong for two years. Disgusted traditionalists insisted that only fools joined the order, Thompson reported, and claimed that idle men and poor hunters provided the mainstay of its festering success.[45] Respectable people, John Tanner explained, condemned the Wabeno as "a false and dangerous religion." Its rituals, such as an obscure rite that involved juggling and swallowing hot stones, differed perversely from those of the Mide and were "usually accompanied by much licentiousness and irregularity."[46] Although the cult apparently had some female members, the Wabeno, unlike the Mide, considered women unfit to touch sacred items.

The record is too incomplete to allow more than speculation on whether women actively worked to protect traditional beliefs against some men's pressures to leave the old ways behind. However, while the evidence is only suggestive, the *windigo*, or *wiitiko*, phenomenon *is* provocative in this regard. The Windigo was a supernatural cannibal monster, a huge and hideous man of ice who stalked the boreal forests of the Cree and Ojibwa, greedily consuming any unfortunates who crossed his path. A human person could also unwittingly "become windigo" (or develop what anthropologists now call windigo psychosis) and crave human flesh to the point of devouring family and friends. James Isham claimed that while Indians would not eat raw meat, they would eat one another when starving; he cited the example of a couple who ate their four children.[47] Not all entered into such behavior involuntarily, however. Duncan Cameron explained that "there are a few who are cannibals by inclination and go about by themselves hunting for Indians with as much industry as if they were hunting animals. The track of one of these is sufficient to make twenty families decamp with all the speed in their power."[48] Prospective victims occasionally distracted the bedeviled windigos with gifts or dosed them with massive quantities of hot tallow.[49] The most reliable solution, however, was to kill the cannibal. The miserable soul would be dispatched stealthily by an axe blow from behind, often at the hands of an anxious wife or relative.

Posthumous proof of the syndrome was that the windigo's heart had turned to ice. To prevent the cannibal from reviving the executioners poured hot tea or water into the chest cavity or in some other manner destroyed the heart. George Nelson described the efforts of one group to dispose of the remains of a young man turned windigo who had told them, as the illness overcame him, that they must be certain to destroy his heart. After his brother and friends had shot him,

> not a drop of blood was seen—*his heart was already formed into Ice*. Here they seized and bound him and with ice chissels and axes set to work to dispatch him. According to his desire they had collected a large pile of dry wood, and laid him upon it. The body was soon

consumed, but the heart remained perfect and entire: it rolled several times off the Pile—they replaced it as often: fear ceased [seized] them—then with their (Ice) chissels they cut and hacked it onto small bits, but yet with difficulty was it consumed!!![50]

Duncan Cameron referred to the case of a Cree woman who killed her husband for fear that he was scheming to bolt down the family (Nelson claimed that windigos turned on their families first). When she saw him drinking blood from an animal's body she took the opportunity to split his head with an axe. The windigo's heart, Cameron attested, was full of ice within his still-warm body.[51]

George Nelson, a fur trader with the North West and Hudson's Bay companies, found that Cree and Northern Ojibwa believed that turning windigo was a punishment from the supernaturals for ignoring or ridiculing ceremonies.[52] This dreadful fate seems to have been viewed as primarily befalling men. As David Thompson explained, "The word Weetego is one of the names of the Evil Spirit and when he gets possession of any Man, (Women are wholly exempt from it) he becomes a Man Eater."[53] Although cases were reported of women suffering from windigo psychosis, the cannibal syndrome was characterized as male; Ruth Landes's study of twentieth-century Ojibwa indicated that only women following male practices were believed susceptible.[54]

The historical record on windigos is vague at best, but it is noteworthy that accounts of the cannibals rose as external pressures and internal conflict increased. Perhaps as gender divergence over commitment to tradition escalated, women sometimes took action against men who flouted tradition in favor of European ways, viewing their individualism as a cannibalism whose consuming hunger threatened everyone's survival. The windigo syndrome might, then, be seen as a metaphor for impending cultural crisis as bands found themselves caught between traditionalism and the mounting pressures of the fur trade and westward expansion.[55]

□ 3 □
THE SECOND PATTERN
Accommodating the Wesleyans

When Great Britain and the United States began a new surge of growth in the early nineteenth century, the Indians of Canada and the Great Lakes area were prime, and vulnerable, targets. The early decades of the century gave rise to a surge of religious fervor that stirred regenerate Protestants to organize to bring the "light and life" of the Gospels to unenlightened peoples the world over. "Christians now have a great deal to do," proclaimed the missionary Sherman Hall:

> They have so much to do to keep their own hearts, and they have much to do also to save sinners and give the gospel to the destitute. A few years ago Christians did (not) know so well as they do now that there were a great many millions of heathens in the world, and that they ought to send them missionaries and the bible. They know it now so well, that they cannot refuse to send the gospel to them, without neglecting a great duty and incurring much guilt.[1]

This duty extended not only to heathens of far-flung lands, but to North American Indians as well. Evangelicals moved quickly to reach those souls.

Before the late eighteenth century, the combined effect of aggressive proselytizing by Roman Catholics, colonial ethno-centrism, and interdenominational rivalry had dampened Prot-estant desires to establish missions in the United States. In the 1790s, however, outbursts of revivalism and religious enthusi-asm radicalized the state of missionary work. Evangelical piety wed orthodoxy to produce a uniquely expansive Protestant Christianity that abandoned the pessimistic rigors of Calvinism to embrace a theology of progressivism and perfectionism.

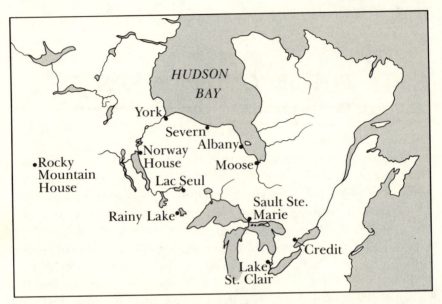

Wesleyan Methodist Missions

One of the first expressions of this new perspective, which embraced Christianity as a dynamic force for world reform, was a systematic effort to create an organized means of spreading the faith. To this end, Protestants formed numerous missionary societies.[2] The American Society for Propagating the Gospel Among the Indians and Others in North America gained legal status in Massachusetts in 1787. The New York Missionary Society, founded in 1796, was the first interdenominational missionary organization in the United States, and the London Missionary Society extended its work to Canada in 1799. Baptists and Congregationalists soon joined the trend, giving rise in 1810 to the interdenominational American Board of Commissioners for Foreign Missions and in 1814 to the Baptist Board of Foreign Missions. The Methodists were relative latecomers to the field: they did not create the Missionary Society of the American Methodist Episcopal Church until 1820.[3]

Native tactics for dealing with renewed missionary sorties varied both with the ebb and flow of proselytization and according to individual community circumstances. Among Canadian peoples, a fluctuating pattern of resistance and accommodation took shape during the nineteenth century. Although the stupefying logistics of penetrating the vast Canadian interior prevented missionaries from making notable inroads in many areas, some native groups in Canada were spurred by economic exigencies or material incentives into contact with the preachers. The responses of these Northern Ojibwa and Cree suggest yet another permutation of gender dynamics within communities.

The contrast in women's and men's attitudes toward Christianity that plagued some of the Jesuit missions had abated by the 1800s. Thereafter, many groups—in particular those near Hudson's Bay Company posts, the St. Lawrence, or the northern shores of the Great Lakes—vociferously opposed initial attempts to convert them, only later to decide that Christianity and "civilization" might help eclipse starvation or invasion by white settlers. Indeed, we find that male shamans and headmen who at first led the opposition often became trusted neophytes, linchpins of the missionary operation. Women, however, are curiously absent from the record. They did not torch missionary homes or fulminate hostilities; indeed, women kept their distance from missionaries. Although they converted infrequently, by the same token it was only on rare occasion that they publicly advocated traditional ways.

The years 1830 to 1870 in Canada appear to have been a transitional phase in Indian-missionary relations. The shift within native communities from often intense opposition to acceptance and even manipulation of Christianity reflected a group's recognition that it was losing the option of continuing independent of white contact. Yet simultaneously, missionaries' relatively few numbers limited their impact and authority in most areas and did not force traditionalists, female or male, into open defense of older ways.

Following the Jesuits' decline in Canada, natives in the interior had little contact with any missionaries until the early nineteenth century, when, in 1818, Roman Catholics established a mission at Pembina on the Red River above the HBC's Fort Douglas. The moment seemed ripe—within three years 267 métis had converted, and many settled near Pembina to farm. The mission's heyday, however, proved brief. In 1823, the company closed Fort Douglas after discovering that it stood in American territory, and local Ojibwa and métis soon claimed the deserted fortress.[4] Missionaries made occasional visits, hoping to bolster the converts' faith, but Major Stephen Long, head of a U.S. War Department expedition that stopped at Pembina in 1823, reported that native women had apparently undermined the priests' efforts. As he put it, métis offspring, "educated by their Indian mothers, have imbibed the roving, unsettled, and indolent habits of Indians."[5] The fur trader Alexander Henry (the younger), who worked out of Pembina in 1801–3 and 1806–8, had found Ojibwa women in the area to be strong-willed and independent, and commented that he had been "vexed at having been obligated to fight with the women" to get their furs in trade.[6]

Long's evocative description of a female convert suggests that native ways may well have seemed a safer course to follow. The expedition was camped at the confluence of the Assiniboin and Red rivers when, in the course of an afternoon, the unsettling sight of a woman haphazardly paddling a canoe and mournfully singing to herself captured their attention. Intrigued, they pressed the residents for information:

> She was a half-breed, whose insanity was supposed to have sprung from a religious melancholy. Being one of those whom the missionaries had converted, she had become very pious, but her intellect was too frail for the doctrines which had been taught to her; in endeavoring to become familiar with them, she had been gradually affected with a malady, which at that time seemed incurable.[7]

Despite the Pembina mission's many problems, news of its initial spectacular success quickly excited Protestant interest in the area. By the 1820s, the Church Missionary Society (of Great Britain) and the Genessee and Canada conferences of the American Methodist Episcopal Church had organized several missions to the Upper Great Lakes.[8] John West's 1820–23 tour of the Canadas for the Church Missionary Society prompted him to publish his travel journal to encourage mission support. "We live in a day when the most distant parts of the earth are opening as the sphere of missionary labors," he reminded his English audience. "The state of the heathen world is becoming better known, and the sympathy of British Christians has been awakened in zealous endeavors to evangelize and soothe its sorrows."[9]

In the 1830s, the Wesleyan Methodist Missionary Society (WMMS) of London opened several missions in Upper Canada and, by invitation, throughout the territory of the Hudson's Bay Company. Although the WMMS missions eventually suffered the common problems of inadequate funding and preparation, it was the first Protestant mission project in North America with both commercial backing and missionaries decently prepared for life in the wilderness. In most areas the WMMS did not draw a large following, but it did elicit positive responses owing to its extensive organization, its ties to the HBC, and economic and environmental changes that made Indians increasingly dependent on the fur trade.

During this period, native subsistence patterns and social relations suffered major upheavals as a result of HBC manipulation of market demands. The 1821 merger of the Hudson's Bay and North West companies had given the HBC a monopoly on the fur trade in Canada. The company's animal conservation policies, combined with large game scarcity, compelled Indians to settle on permanent family territories and to shift their subsistence base to small game and fish. Forced to locate near company posts for access to firearms and food during times of famine, by the 1840s many Ojibwa and Cree found that the HBC played a central role in their lives.[10]

When the hymn-singing, HBC-backed Wesleyans debarked in 1833, native society was particularly susceptible to their appeal, and so the earliest years of missions to Ojibwa and Cree in Upper Canada seemed quite promising. This favorable situation was due largely to the earlier proselytizing by Kahkewakwonaby (Peter Jones), son of a Welsh surveyor and an Ojibwa woman, educated in English schools. In 1825, two years after his own conversion to Methodism, Jones became an exhorter, or lay preacher. One of his first moves was to convince members of his own Mississauga (Eastern Ojibwa) band to join in the rousing camp meetings at Grand River. Within four years, at the request of relatives, he had established a mission at Snake and Yellowhead islands on Lake Simcoe.[11]

North American Methodist missions had been under the auspices of the Methodist Episcopal Church of the United States, an arrangement made by the American and British churches in 1820 (without the consent of Canadian Methodists).[12] When American Methodists turned their Indian missions in Canada over to the recently formed Canada Conference in 1824, British Wesleyans declared that the 1820 agreement was void and claimed that the way was now clear for British evangelizing. In response, the Canada Conference hurried to open new Indian missions; it also sent Peter Jones and George Ryerson, a white Canadian minister, to tour England in 1831 and muster support.[13] The conference's hopes were dashed, however, when the government of Upper Canada revised its Indian Department policies and, in 1832, invited the British Wesleyans to begin work among Canadian Indians. To avoid intrachurch conflict, British and Canadians merged forces in Canada, and in 1833 the Wesleyan Methodist Missionary Society of London took over the Canadian Indian missions.[14]

The arrival of Thomas Turner at St. Clair at the southern tip of Lake Huron that year signaled the beginning of WMMS missionary efforts in Upper Canada along the St. Lawrence River and eastern Great Lakes.[15] Initially, Turner felt himself a failure. Charging that the adults drank too much to allow conversion, he suggested to the society that it would be more productive to concentrate on the children—"the rising generation."[16] By January 1834, however, his spirits had lifted. "A short time ago a circumstance occured here which led me to hope that the prejudices of the Indians are in some degree wearing off," Turner informed society secretary Robert Alder in London. "Trivial indeed it may appear to many, but to a missionary living among pure pagans as these Indians are, even such an incident is not without interest." The occasion was the funeral of a young man who had drowned during an epileptic seizure. When Wawanosh, the local band's spokesperson, asked Turner to pray before they lowered the coffin, the minister at first demurred, afraid the others would stop him. Finally, "as I soon observed that the other Chiefs, and nearly all the men who were present joined with Waywaynosh in his request I consented, and during prayer both men and women were silent and attentive."[17] Turner was sure that the men's insistence on Christian prayers gave new life to his work.

Turner and his successors, like the Jesuits, focused their energies on wooing men into the fold. While they did not discount the value of female souls, it was male conversions that brought the thrill of success. In 1835 Joseph Stinson, general superintendent of missions, could report to the secretary of the WMMS that "there is amongst our Indians an increasing number of sensible, pious, enterprising young men, who are exerting themselves to promote the spiritual interests of their red brethren in the wilderness." Many of the most important men, the old "Pow Wows," he exulted, were "now as zealous in forwarding as they were formerly in opposing the work of the Lord."[18] The missionaries marshaled their examples: one man converted and immediately abandoned his medicine bundle; Sault, a shaman from the River St. Clair band and "one of the most wicked men in the tribe," assured Stinson that upon converting he "bade farewell to my master, the Devil and broke [my] whiskey bottle as a token."[19] Old Shuctahgun, a Midewiwin shaman from St. Clair, eagerly embraced Christianity and exhorted his band to accept the new religion. The Grand River mission boasted more than a hundred members in the society, including some "truly pious and happy" females.[20]

This was indeed a dramatic reversal of initial reactions. When, for example, the superintendent of Indians suggested a mission settlement on Walpole Island, the local band had responded that the Great Spirit wanted them as they were and would have given them books if it wanted natives to have them. "Is it just and prudent that we who have held so long after the customs and traditions of our forefathers, should all at once jump at another kind of religion that is so different from ours?" Paghegezhegwaish and Sharlow asked. "No, we will never be so foolish as this. We will never venture to run such a great risk. Who knows but what the Munadoo (gods) would be angry with us for abandoning our old ways."[21]

But exuberant Methodist preaching apparently soon swayed them: "No sooner did they feel the power of the Spirit of God resting upon them, than they began to desire to improve in their temporal ambitions." At Credit, Grape Island, Rice Lake,

St. Clair, and other sites, Ojibwa rapidly converted and settled into permanent villages.[22] From Sault Ste. Marie, James Evans claimed that several chiefs seemed quite taken by Methodism. "I think we have a good prospect for the Sault," he wrote Stinson from Hayward's Sound. "The old chief has visited us and complains of not having any missionary or teacher." Evans also rejoiced in an auspicious harvest of souls: "We yesterday Baptized six men one woman and three children."[23] Several months later, Evans, writing to his family from Mishebegwadoong, regaled them with more news of the Sault's bright future:

> Yesterday the head chief of the tribe, a fine looking fellow, arrived and we were highly gratified in seeing him leading all his people to our wiggewaum in the evening in order to hear of the "good way." . . . I am anxiously looking for their return in the spring as the Chief informs us that his people will desire to be instructed and that they will do anything which God's servants direct them to do.[24]

The mission drew not only chiefs, but supposedly unsalvageable men, even windigos, as well. "We had in our congregation last Sunday an Indian cannibal," Evans told his wife and daughter. "It is well known that he and an old woman (a witch looking character) killed and eat two Frenchmen about two years ago, he is a sour savage looking fellow and looks as though he could eat anything. He however declared his intention to strive to serve the Great Spirit and acknowledged that he has been a very wicked man."[25] The missionaries conceded that the men felt forced by circumstances to accept Christianity: "It is useless for us to go on in our *old ways* any longer," Stinson quoted them as saying; "we shall all have to become Christians."[26] In this spirit, one Ojibwa delegation solicited the WMMS for a missionary, presenting a letter signed by sixty-five members of their village: "We Indians living at Salt Springs on the Grand River, have been considering what we should do now. Our minds are that we should ask Mr. Stinson to send us a Missionary, because we wish to be English Methodists. These are our own thoughts, and to show Mr. Stinson what we wish, we have signed our names to this paper."[27]

Viewing such requests as auguries of victory, the Wesleyans increased their activity during the late 1830s. Under their guidance approximately one thousand Ojibwa had established settled communities and "applied themselves with success to the arts of civilized life" by 1837. Although the natives were not particularly apt farmers or artisans, the missionaries contended that, nevertheless, they were moving along the path to civilization. "The Christian Indian is learning to appreciate the advantages connected with a fixed habitation. He has a *home*, and a domestic Altar on which 'Prayer is daily set forth as incense.' He has a sanctuary in which he worships . . . and a School for the instruction of his children."[28]

Schools figured prominently in the Upper Canada missions: by removing children from "their imperfectly civilized parents," Methodists planned to set Indian youth firmly on the road to Christianity and away from barbarism. Robert Alder, WMMS secretary, envisioned a system that initiated children into the practical joys of civilization. In particular, he emphasized the need to inculcate girls with the domestic values of nineteenth-century British womanhood, so that they could bring future generations of the race with them. "The Boys would be instructed in a knowledge of useful mechanical arts; and what is greatly to be desired, as being of immense importance in its influence on the future improvement of the Indians, the female portion of the children would be well instructed, not merely in reading and writing, but in the performance of domestic duties."[29]

The WMMS soon started a farm and industrial school at Alderville at Rice Lake (Ontario) in 1837. The school was small, with twelve to fifteen pupils, the schedule rigorous, and the girls' training relentless in focus:

> They rise during the winter at *five* o'clock: and in summer at *one half past four*. The girls proceed to milk the cows: then prepare the breakfast: attend family prayers; and hear a lecture, or exposition on a portion of the Scriptures—the singing, and all the exercises are in English. The girls then set the cheese; and do housework—at nine a.m. they go into school—at noon dinner and at *half-past one* p.m.: school recommenses: then as above mentioned, needle-

work—school closes at *half-past four p.m.*. At five, supper—at six, milking the cows prayers at *eight p.m.*: at half-past eight, they retire to rest.[30]

The schoolmasters did not record the children's response to this experience, but one can imagine that daily submission to such rigid schedules, combined with removal from their mothers and fathers, was a grueling ordeal for many.

Despite the program's strictness, however, the Indian Industrial School was popular with local Ojibwa. In 1848, they voted to put part of their annuities toward its support, in the not unsubstantial amount of £345.12.8. By the following year twenty-six students were enrolled, and the Ojibwa granted deed to two hundred acres to the school.[31] Christian and "wild" Indians alike—increasingly "aliens and outcasts in those regions over which their fathers bore undisputed sway"—obligingly sent their children to schools for instruction.[32]

The WMMS's next move was to send James Evans, Thomas Hurlburt, and two native preachers, Shawdais (John Sunday) and Pahtahsega (Peter Jacobs), on an exploratory journey into the northwest interior of Canada. Their errand resulted in an unprecedented collaboration of the WMMS with the Hudson's Bay Company, targeting Indians between Hudson Bay and the Rocky Mountains.[33] The HBC traditionally had prohibited its employees or others in its territory from instructing Indians in religion, under pain of dismissal.[34] In 1839, however, the company decided that Christianity would benefit both Indians and the HBC, and so it reversed its antievangelization policy.

By this time, the land and people between Churchill River and James Bay had been exhausted by alien diseases, overhunting, and famine. As early as 1820, John West observed that the Swampy Cree at York Factory seemed worn out and suffering.[35] Indians from the York Factory area had begun to migrate to the more hospitable environment and higher wages of Red River. It was the company's hope that conversion would persuade them (particularly the Home Guard Cree who provisioned the HBC) to remain instead near their traditional northern hunting grounds. Roman Catholics and Anglicans, however, disregarded the company's desires and contentiously encouraged converts to relocate near their Red River missions.

Drawn by the work-discipline theology of the Wesleyans, the HBC directors determined that Methodism could best convince natives to remain in the area and trap more regularly and efficiently.[36] The company therefore offered travel and maintenance to WMMS missionaries coming into the country from England and granted them rank equivalent to wintering partner, or commissioned officer.[37]

The WMMS seized the opportunity, and in 1840 James Evans and three young British ministers ventured into the vast expanse of the Canadian northwest, covering all together a territory more than fifteen hundred miles across. Evans installed himself at Norway House on Lake Winnipeg, George Barnley at Moose Fort on James Bay, William Mason on Lac la Pluie (called Rainy Lake by the British), and Robert Rundle at Rocky Mountain House in present-day Alberta. The following year Thomas Hurlburt, Pahtahsega (hereafter referred to by his WMMS signature, Peter Jacobs) and Shahwahnegezhik (Henry E. Steinhauer), an Ojibwa lay preacher from the Credit mission, joined the HBC territory missions.[38]

The missionaries set up shop within or just outside the HBC posts; as agreed, the company provided accommodations in its own quarters, with the promise of a separate establishment when feasible. The ministers found, however, that fulfillment of this pledge could require a great deal of prodding.[39] Housing soon became an issue, since the Wesleyans, like most nineteenth-century Protestant missionaries, believed that their own family lives must provide models of Christian domesticity for heathens. This required, of course, not only that they be married, but also that their mates be present and adequate to the rigors of life in the bush. James Evans's brother, Ephraim, set forth the requisite attributes of a married woman missionary: "The *wives* should be of the right stamp. Not nervous timid creatures who dare not let their husbands go from home—nor ladies unaccustomed to practical housekeeping. They must be *willing* to put up with much inconvenience, and to look for their reward in a world from which they shall see the future fruits of cheerful endurance of hardship."[40]

Clearly these were to be women of character and determination who would be helpmeets to their spouses in and out of chapel and classroom. Moreover, the very responsibilities of their daily lives would guide Indian females toward Christian womanhood.[41] Some women, such as those married to George Barnley and Henry Steinhauer, or Eliza Field Jones, an Englishwoman married to Peter Jones, taught classes and prayed with Indians; but most found their time consumed by child care, frequent illness, and domestic chores made more difficult by the harsh climate.[42] Their sporadic attempts to teach native women to sew and knit apparently met with little success. One of John Sinclair's reports suggested that Indian women in the bush deliberately discouraged Home Guard women at the posts from collaborating with the missionaries. Cree women at the mission station refused to cooperate in the manufacture of handiwork to sell in England. "The minds of the women are so much prejudiced by our country ladies [Indian women living in the bush]," Sinclair claimed, "that they care very little of doing any work for us, or for anyone else whom they know is sending home work to England."[43]

While living examples of the Christian family were important, the mission wives' activities did not figure centrally in the WMMS plan. Rather, the society depended on preaching and hymnals and scriptural excerpts in Ojibwa or Cree syllabics, often printed laboriously on small hand presses at the missions, to broadcast the good word. Because the HBC originally objected to the use of the press for fear that a newspaper might work against the company's interests, the WMMS spent considerable effort to gain permission to print at the missions. In the interim the missionaries were quite innovative. James Evans, for example, printed on birch bark using original type made from tea chest lead or bullets, while at Moose Factory George Barnley carved the type out of plaster of Paris blocks.[44]

Proselytizing was to be done not only by English missionaries, but also by native preachers such as Jacobs and Steinhauer. Thomas Hurlburt reported to Secretary Alder from Fort Pic on Lake Superior, "It will be necessary for white men to oversee the work in that country but it is my conviction that we must look to our native agents, as the great & immediate instrument, in the conversion of the heathen."[45] Hurlburt, who had a good command of Ojibwa language and mythology, recognized the strength of native beliefs and insisted that one must understand them to supplant them. Knowledge of native ways, he wrote, "gives the missionary the power of combatting them in their strongholds. For as ignorant as they are they have a system of Demonology of their own which in many or most cases has a strong hold on their feelings."[46] Native preachers therefore had the inside track on traditional religion.

In Rupert's Land in the 1840s, both English and native missionaries envisioned a field as ripe for spiritual harvest as had been those of Jones and Turner in Upper Canada. Instead they confronted an Indian "demonology" to which whole bands of Ojibwa and Cree adhered, even after several years of preaching. Henry Steinhauer discovered that although an Indian might admire his ability to read the Bible, in the case of a Rainy Lake chief (and others), "he manifested no desire to learn nor did he at all wish to become acquainted with the principle of Christianity."[47] And a frustrated Peter Jacobs furiously denounced the obstinacy of the local Indians in a report from Fort Alexander in 1841:

> I have found them to be very wicked, and that they are greates[t] blackguards that I ever have seen; and that they have not the least desire of becoming Christians. I have preached the word of God to them time after time: and that I now feel cleare of their blood. and they will now go to the Devil they will go there, with their eyes open. and that I have told them so. However one of them has given me his councent to become a Christian.[48]

By 1848, however, Jacobs still had not made much headway. He targeted Rainy Lake as the "headquarters of Heathenism of the surrounding Country" and blamed this on local "conjurers," or Midewiwin shamans.[49] These practitioners commanded large followings and, unlike shamans at the Credit and St. Clair missions in Upper Canada, vigorously fought all of Jacobs's efforts to promote Christianity. With the censure of an apostate, he repeatedly complained that their loyalty to tradition grew out of greed and self-interest in maintaining lucrative customs:

> Indians fear & tremble before them many an Indian comes from afar to be initiated in the conjuring arts that comes with guns, [word illegible], blankets, cloths, traps, knives & dogs & gives all the foregoing articles to the head-conjurors for being initiated in the secret arts of Conjuring high & indeed some of these new-comers

have stripped themselves & their families entirely naked. In return for these goods the Conjurers teach them sleight hand &, giving them, a few herbs and making them out as medicines of great virtues & frequently what the conjurers give is not worth more than a shilling or two. By this deceiving way of the Conjurers they accumulate good fortunes for themselves & for their families. These are the reasons that the head-conjurers are bitterly opposed to Christianity because Christianity strikes at the roots of their interests. I am sorry to say that the Lac La Pluie Indians are really mad in their idolatrous worship.[50]

In some instances, a community's fears for its own well-being apparently motivated widespread opposition to the missionaries. When the beleaguered Jacobs attempted a mission at Munedoo Rapids in 1849, his efforts were an unconditional failure. "The majority of the Indians are inimical to the establishment of a mission," he commented bitterly, "and will continue to be so."[51] These Ojibwa did not find Methodism a compelling substitute for traditional beliefs and feared that Jacobs's presence would offend the manitous of the fish, driving them away. Moreover, Jacobs was convinced that those sympathetic to his efforts were really hoping to improve their material rather than spiritual conditions:

> The principle reasons that illustrate the repugnance of these Indians for the establishment of a mission are as follows. First. they hate Christianity from the bottom of their hearts because pure Christianity strikes at the very root of their heathenism. Secondly. They think that if a Mission was established at either of the two great fisheries, the Munedoo Rapids & Kange-wahnoong, which are about four miles apart, the fish would leave the rapids—a vain excuse this is. The few that are inclined to have a mission there are not really religiously disposed, but I am afraid nothing but worldly motives is all that they have in view. And to say the real truth, I have no confidence in these fellows at all, for they are a very deceitful tribe.[52]

Other bands remained at best ambivalent, uncertain whether Christianity was worth the risk. Older people at Lac Seul, 150 miles northeast of Jacobs's Rainy Lake mission, seemed receptive at first. They agreed to let him instruct their children but insisted that they themselves were "too old and too ignorant" for his preaching. When two years of hard work produced no visible results, Jacobs blamed his failure on the old people's self-interest. Because they felt that conversion would be a great favor to Jacobs, they expected equal compensation in food and clothing. When Jacobs made no attempt to supply these items as incentive, "they manifested a great disappointment" and continued with their own practices.[53]

Similarly, the hostile shamans at Rainy Lake informed Jacobs in July 1848 that they would convert if he promised to ordain them. He was certain, however, that they would just use their Christian ministerial positions to recoup the losses incurred when the lucrative Midewiwin training was discontinued. Incensed, he refused to ordain them, a move that only aroused further hostility toward the mission. But the conjurers later decided that in the long run "the white man & his religion are too great to be opposed by a weak set like ourselves" and pragmatically opted to send their children for instruction.[54]

This pattern of initial resistance followed by a degree of acquiescence to Wesleyan efforts probably resulted from the combined impact of deteriorating economic conditions and the HBC's support of the missions. In the late 1840s and into the 1850s, famine was a frequent threat. Jacobs reported that in his area wild rice crops were failing, disease had decimated the rabbit population, and fish were scarce as well. "In this critical condition of the Indians," he observed, "they begin to talk of embracing civilization & Christianity. But when the months of May & June comes, the Season when they get plenty of Sturgeon, all their fair promises will be sunk in oblivion."[55]

Thomas Hurlburt also reported widespread hunger and suffering among the Indians in the vicinity of Fort Pic, but blamed this situation on contact with whites. "The Indians are diminished in number & reduced to the lowest state of wretchedness & dependence. This may be imputed to the introduction of fire arms into the country," he claimed, "& to the competition between the two rival trading companies, when the poor indian was urged by his thirst of ardent spirits to make wanton destruction of his only means of subsistence." These circumstances, he concluded, made these the most "docile" Indians he had ever met.[56]

The demands of the fur trade were great. William Mason complained that autumn trapping hampered the practice of Christianity, and overwhelming debts to the fur companies allowed the Cree no escape. "What a wretched system is this debt work!—The Indian is much enslaved by it," he explained, "yet so long accustomed to the system that he values not the time—labour—& situations he endures while attempting to discharge his debts."[57] Hunters were gone for so long that any good impressions of Christianity wore thin. To combat this circumstance, Mason resorted to bribing natives to stay at the mission. He was aided in this effort by their constant hunger: on one occasion he doled out more than two thousand fish in a fortnight to keep them fed. George Barnley, too, learned to exploit the situation; when starving Indians came into Moose Factory for food, he seized the moment and preached to them, viewing it as a God-given chance to proselytize. The use of books was seen as another means of combating the problem of time not spent with missionaries when in the bush: "They love their books & constantly read when out hunting," Mason reported. Mason distributed more than three hundred copies of "No. 1 Conference Catechism with Lord's Prayer."[58]

Hunters engaged by the HBC apparently soon realized that conversion, or at least a receptive attitude toward the missionaries, was a productive and reasonable tactic. Group leaders came under a great deal of pressure from both the government and missionaries to accept Christianity for their bands, and they knew that if they converted they could maintain their authority as Methodist class leaders or preachers.[59] Peter Jacobs's negotiations with the shamans and chiefs at Rainy Lake indicated clearly the importance to them of retaining status. Although the Rainy Lake Ojibwa were an ongoing source of frustration for the long-suffering Jacobs, by 1849 a number of headmen had requested that he help them take the first steps to becoming educated and "civilized."[60]

Missionaries throughout the interior reported that chiefs and shamans had converted, abandoning their medicine bundles for the Gospels. Some gave up their "idols, medicine, drums &c&c," others renounced rum, and a number even included their youngest wives among the castoffs; Mason, for example, included two "repudiated wives" on his 1848 census of Rossville mission.[61] One man, an "apostle of the false Indian prophet" of Beaver River, had traveled to Norway House with the intention of swaying the local Cree to reject the missionaries and join the revitalization movement. But only the slightest exposure to William Mason's charismatic oratory sent him home apparently determined instead to bring his relatives to Christianity.[62]

Rossville at Norway House was probably the most successful of the WMMS Rupert's Land missions. Fifty to seventy students usually attended the school, which was established by James Evans. In 1848, Rossville had a Christian village of thirty-nine converted families. (The numbers would have been even greater if not for the devastation of the 1846–47 smallpox and measles epidemics.) Moreover, the station boasted seven native preachers. Despite William Mason's belief that the setting retarded Christianity and civilization (the climate was too severe for agriculture and dogs devoured the imported cattle), by 1852 the mission, now boasting 107 full church members, appeared to be flourishing.[63] Mason reported from York Factory that year that "heathenism has received its death blow and falls before the power & influence of the Gospel, priestly incantations and indian juggling have ceased. The conjurers themselves are asking for baptism at the hands of the Missionaries." During the same month he baptized the five children of the few remaining non-Christian chiefs at Oxford House.[64] Although he proved to be overly optimistic in his estimates of Methodism's success among Cree communities, Mason was convinced that the majority of influential men in the area had converted.

These men not only converted, but they also insisted that their families be baptized. In particular, they wanted their sons and grandsons received into the church. One fellow consigned his medicine bundle with its manitous to James Evans and in return demanded of Peter Jacobs that his wife and unborn child be accepted too. "This is the station of his speech to me," Jacobs reported:

> I have now given my whole heart to God. I now deliver up my heathen gods [medicine bundles] to you. and do with them as you please. (I have given them to Brother Evans and I think he will

send them to you.) And here is my wife I wish her to go to heaven with me; and that she has a little Indian with her that is to be born within a month or two. I also give this child to the Lord. and I hope you will take and make it happy. and you must baptize it for he must also be a Christian. So I have now given my whole heart and my wife and my child to the Lord, now pray for me.[65]

Other men too, such as an Ojibwa chief from Walpole Island, also gave their children for instruction, or even sent them for training at the Wesleyan Industrial School at Mt. Elgin. In the final analysis, though, Old Batosh, a mixed-blood Cree, was undoubtedly the most generous initiate: he promised to commit his entire retinue of more than sixty children and grandchildren to Mason's spiritual guidance.[66]

The shift in male attitudes from opposition to acceptance (whether for spiritual or practical reasons) has been interpreted as an indication of widespread and rapid adoption of Christianity. There is little evidence, however, that women actively sought to join in the conversion trend.[67] While the missionaries did not always specify converts' gender, males represented a clear majority of the baptisms reported in the WMMS correspondence. Of the conversions in which the convert's sex was specifically stated, thirty-four of fifty (68 percent) adult conversions were male.

Only on rare occasions did women demonstrate open resistance; in general their responses are obscure in the mission record. Undoubtedly, Western preconceptions of native women helped shape women's experiences with Methodist evangelicals and Christianity. Developing concepts of domesticity and femininity among the middle and upper classes in England and the United States in the nineteenth century rendered woman spiritually and morally powerful only if she devoted herself wholly to the care of home and family. Frail and nervous, ruled by emotion, a "prisoner of her reproductive system," the Christian woman knew her place and joyfully submitted to her husband's will.[68] Although her focus was on bearing and raising children, she was not a sexual creature. Indeed, most male medical practitioners and health reformers insisted that a real woman did not desire regular sexual activity, and that those who did sapped male strength and unnaturally increased their own. On the contrary, feminine morality was based on chastity and modesty.[69]

Indian women's independence, socially and sexually, horrified the Wesleyan missionaries as it had the Jesuits. The Methodist perspective was perhaps even more rigid, however. Evangelicals viewed human existence as an ongoing struggle between the conscience and the physical self; because they were basically hostile to the temptations of the flesh, they regarded sexuality and the body with a wariness verging on fear.[70] James Evans's report about conditions at the St. Clair mission indicates his attitude about native women clearly. Although he believed that the men were often idle or drunk, the women, he said, were particularly debauched, for "their very sex enabled them to be more audaciously obscene."[71]

Methodists in both Britain and the United States were debating the issue of female education in the 1840s. James Dixon, a British Wesleyan minister who toured Methodist churches in Canada and the United States during that decade, made a strong case for the need to instruct women. He stated the usual commonplace about women's role in forming the character of the next generation, but he also made a point that must have struck home in a period fraught with interdenominational rivalry: educating women was a way to combat the growth of the Catholic church. "The women are always the objects of attention with the Popish church. . . . The moral force of the Popery, so long exercised in the world, has been accomplished very much through the societies formed in various ways to influence, to educate, and then to employ, women, for the furtherance of its objectives."[72]

This was a sticky issue, for, like the Jesuits, the Wesleyans insisted that missionaries have but limited interaction with native women. Evangelists received specific instructions on this matter, such as those sent to George Barnley shortly after his arrival at Moose Factory in March 1840 on how to behave with native women:

> Keep at the utmost distance from all trifling and levity in your intercourse with young persons, more especially with females. Take no liberties with them. Converse with them very sparingly

and only for religious purposes; even then do not converse with them alone. Be above suspicion. Beware of the half cast females— the daughters of Europeans by native women. Forget not that the thought of foolishness is sin.[73]

As a result, women often had only minimal contact with WMMS missionaries. To be sure, the Wesleyans did attract some female converts, but in these cases the women seem to have based their decision on practical rather than spiritual factors. Certainly few women claimed spiritual rebirth, although group conversions following camp meetings may indicate instances when women were swept up emotionally. In general, however, familial circumstances apparently governed a woman's decision to convert. For example, Thomas Woolsey reported from Edmonton House in 1858 that he had baptized Joseph La Patack, an important Cree chief, and his wife. Joseph obviously commanded more notice and support than his unnamed wife. "[His] subsequent deportment," Woolsey observed with satisfaction, "has convinced me and others that I had not mistaken the sincerity of Joseph La Patack's profession at his baptism."[74] Woolsey never commented on the woman's commitment, and one suspects that she was simply part of a mandatory family conversion, like some other wives—for example, Mrs. Wawanosh, wife of a head chief at St. Clair mission—and many children. One woman to whom the missionaries did direct attention, however, was Mary Ann Morrison, the Cree wife of a Scots employee of the HBC at Norway House. A model Christian, her happy deathbed scene warmed Charles Stringfellow's heart: "she literally went home to God rejoicing," declaring that " 'Christianity has done me good.' "[75]

Some women requested baptism following a brush with death—their own or that of loved ones. In the early years of the Credit mission, a woman saved at a camp meeting revealed that she had recently lost several children. With touching symbolism she described her conversion experience: "For this last week, I have been filling, & filling, but that time [the prayer meeting] I thought I should have burst."[76] Margaret Sohia, of the Rossville mission at Norway House, asked for instruction following her recovery from a severe illness. She told Stringfellow, the missionary, that she trusted in Jesus and would even die if God so wished.[77]

Conversion, though, was no guarantee of a woman's permanent acceptance of Christianity. Occasionally they backslid openly, abandoning Methodism to regain sexual or marital freedom. One of the most distressing cases to the missionaries was that of a woman from Rossville who had led an exemplary Christian life. Nevertheless, she remained torn between the old ways and the new, and in the end she left Rossville to return to' her relatives and traditional beliefs, later dying with the question of her "doom" unanswered in the missionaries' minds.[78]

Only a few women publicly opposed the Wesleyans, and rather flamboyantly. George Barnley attributed the exuberant but ephemeral success of a prophetic movement at Moose Factory and York Fort in 1843 to the fact that "a missionary zeal was awakened in the bosoms of an old woman and a youth who took up their residence among the Albany Indians, and soon introduced their chart, with all the enchanting revelations of the new system, and the poor people were almost universally carried away with the delusion."[79] According to the ministers, the movement originated in the discontent of two male shamans at Fort Severn who blamed Christianity for their declining influence, although HBC records indicate that the leader was a Home Guard Cree from York Fort who advocated communal distribution of meat and the destruction of dogs used to haul for the company. Transported by visions of a fantastic Indian heaven replete with fat deer and a fabulous mansion closed to whites, the woman and her young helper mesmerized the local Cree.[80]

HBC officers reported to Governor George Simpson that the old woman's success in propagating the new beliefs had turned the Indians lazy—an intolerable situation for the profit-oriented Englishmen, who retaliated by spreading the rumor that Abishabis, the original visionary, was a windigo. The chief trader at Albany, G. Pramston, labeled Abishabis a fraud, and the company then imprisoned, tried, and condemned him at Fort Severn. A hatchet blow from behind (classic windigo execution) finished Abishabis's prophetic quest. In a dramatic finale to the episode, company officers forced the woman and boy to toss their cultic paraphernalia into a bonfire before an assemblage of Cree and HBC employees.[81]

In another case, "Our Queen Dowager down the river" drove poor Peter Jacobs nearly to despair in his struggle to convert the Rainy Lake Ojibwa (whom he likened to "the Jews of old. 'behold this people is a stiffnecked people' "). This duplicitous woman, he complained, "gave me many encouragements, saying again and again that 'not only herself,' but her people would soon become Christians. Now during the past year she also took it in her head to give her hand and heart to a man who had a wife already." Jacobs, devastated by the woman's rejection of Christianity and the principles of monogamy that he had tried to teach her, was convinced that she had woefully damaged his accomplishments.[82]

Overall, however, the tenor of women's responses to WMMS missionaries might almost be called demure. There was no clear pattern of acceptance or rejection; women seldom openly resisted the Wesleyans, but, unlike men, neither did they seek out religious or secular instruction. This was a marked contrast to the antagonism encountered by the Jesuits or by missionaries working in the late 1700s and early decades of the 1800s. During the Wesleyans' tenure, indeed, there was little evidence of the pattern described by David Thompson and others of women's traditionalism leading to incipient gender conflict in communities that had come under European influence.

The ambiguous character of female response appears to rise from two features of this period: the shifting nature of native life in mid-nineteenth-century Canada and the Wesleyans' perspective on the importance of women to their mission. Although individual men resisted conversion, the number of shamans and leaders who did convert suggests that Christianity exercised greater appeal to males, who found it necessary for maintaining a working relationship with the Hudson's Bay Company. As conditions in Rupert's Land and Upper Canada grew increasingly desperate for Indians, limiting their autonomy and increasing interaction with and economic dependence on whites, women may well have realized that open antagonism toward missionaries only worsened the situation; thus they tempered their responses so as to protect community relations with the HBC. In essence, they found that it was counter-productive to oppose the missionaries.

Although the Wesleyan missionaries did not face pronounced resistance from women, their success was nonetheless limited. The WMMS missions withered away, fraught with problems and neglected by London as internal struggles for reform absorbed Methodists in England. James Evans returned to England in 1846, ostensibly to repair his failing health, but he left behind a string of accusations asserting that he had intimidated Indian girls into sexual relations with him. Ironically, he died upon his arrival in London, but his fellow missionaries continued to debate the matter of his innocence for years.[83]

Several ministers relinquished their posts out of concern for the well-being of their wives. Childbirth and illness incapacitated George Barnley's wife and, he explained, "acting on a naturally excitable temperament produce[d] a state of nervousness, & depression almost insupportable to herself, & of course very distressing to me."[84] When the situation became unbearable, the Barnleys left Moose Factory and returned to England without awaiting WMMS approval for vacating the mission. Peter Jacobs's wife also went into decline in the hostile environment of Rainy Lake. "She is pining away, very fast," he anxiously reported; "whether this is the cause of the troubles we now have or from the disappointment of not going to Canada I cannot tell; when I ask her the cause of her pining away she says nothing."[85] Of the group of missionaries whose tenure began following the transfer of the missions to the Canadians, perhaps most striking was the situation of Robert Brooking's wife. Following their return to Canada from Rossville, Enoch Wood, missionary superintendent of the Canada Conference, reported that "Mrs. B. is much altered, having a depressed, squaw-like appearance. Their daughter has been neglected. She is as wild as a deer. . . . I feel somewhat interested to see the changes."[86]

Moreover, the Hudson's Bay Company had become disenchanted with the Methodists' inability to maintain their missions, and Governor Simpson went so far as to suggest to Enoch Wood that HBC territories were no longer a desirable field for Methodist efforts. In self-defense, Wood told the WMMS that the company wanted the Methodists out of its lands, that it now viewed the missionaries' efforts as a deterrent to economic gain.[87] By 1852, William Mason was the only Wesleyan missionary in Rupert's Land; alone, he could not meet the spiritual needs of his sparse and widely spread flock. Discouraged by lack of support, Mason transferred to the Church of England's Christian Missionary Society (which had tried to have all the WMMS missions transferred to its jurisdiction) in 1854 and moved from the area.[88]

That same year, the WMMS turned over the Rupert's Land missions to the Canada Conference. Thomas Woolsey, along with Robert Brooking, Charles Stringfellow, and Henry Steinhauer, participated in this fresh start. But despite the new attempt, the Rupert's Land missions made little headway. The seriousness of the situation became clear when Woolsey, at Victoria mission in present-day Alberta, received a letter from William Os-ke-maw-gweyan and three other men. These Stone Indians from Goose River claimed that the Wesleyans "threw us away," leaving them to struggle, in Woolsey's words, "as sheep without a shepherd."[89] Indeed, the Wesleyans were unable to provide them with any missionary, and the Canadian Methodists gradually abandoned the Northern Ojibwa and Cree in favor of domestic proselytizing.[90]

4

THE THIRD PATTERN
Unity

South of Rupert's Land, Ojibwa communities in the Upper Great Lakes area fluctuated more visibly in their stance toward evangelicals than did the Cree and Northern Ojibwa. Throughout the first half of the nineteenth century, Southeastern and Southwestern Ojibwa responded to mission efforts with an inquisitive ambivalence that eventually turned to suspicion and hostility. While they initially received the young Presbyterian and Congregational missionaries with interest, they eventually came to view them as agents of the federal government—forerunners of white settlers determined to deprive Indians of land and living.

American Protestant interest in proselytizing Ojibwa and other native groups in the early 1800s arose in part from the theory of "disinterested benevolence," a concept based on a universal affection (or love) for all intelligent beings demanded by God of humans. Mission work seemed a natural expression of this benevolence: love compelled missionaries to fight for the salvation of the heathen world.[1] By 1820, disinterested benevolence was the slogan of the mission effort, as Rev. Daniel Haskell made clear in his introduction to fur trader Daniel William Harmon's Canadian travel journal:

> The time is rapidly coming, when christian benevolence will emulate the activity and perseverance, which have long been displayed in commercial enterprises; when no country will remain unexplored by the heralds of the cross, where immortal souls are shrouded in the darkness of heathenism, and are persisting for lack of vision. The wandering and benighted sons of our own forests shall not be overlooked.... The Indian tribes, whose

CANADA

UNITED
STATES   La
            Pointe
Leech L.
    Odanah   Lac de   Mackinac   Sault Ste. Marie
Round L.   Flambeau
        Lac Court   Cross Village
        Oreilles   Omena   Little
                                     Traverse
            WISCONSIN
                                Grand
MINNESOTA   Traverse

                          MICHIGAN
                    Lake St. Clair

Protestant Missions in the Great Lakes Area

condition is unfolded in this work, have claims upon Christian compassion.[2]

This new advocacy for Native American missions closely paralleled social, economic, and political developments in the early nineteenth century. Growing international commerce broadened the American market, and, in time-honored tradition, traders felicitously cultivated new sources of converts for missionaries. Moreover, the expanding market resulted in an increased prosperity that made it seem not just feasible but desirable to fund missions. Haskell even ventured to propose an organization staffed jointly by missionaries and the North West Company (Daniel Harmon's employer) to bring Christianity and civilization to the Indians. This would, he confidently stated, "with much less trouble and even expense to them, accomplish the object which the Company have in view, than any establishment which they could independently make; and which would, at the same time, have a most auspicious bearing upon the religious interests of the tribes of the N.W. Country."[3] Budding nationalism combined with economic growth to promote rapid geographic expansion as the United States began to finance expeditions to the western lands in order to eliminate Great Britain and France as territorial rivals. The ultimate goal, of course, was to secure new territory, but in the process the nation engulfed Indians as well, and to many Americans it was evident that the natives would have to be civilized and Christianized.

Henry Schoolcraft, a government Indian agent, is an excellent example of one who operated under this moral obligation. In 1832, Schoolcraft organized an expedition to map the course of the Mississippi River and contact the Ojibwa (Chippewa) of northern Minnesota. As a matter of course, his staffing request to the U.S. Office of Indian Affairs included both a missionary and an engineer for mapmaking. In a letter to the corresponding secretary of the American Board of Commissioners for Foreign Missions (ABCFM), Schoolcraft explained why he believed that a minister should participate in the expedition: "Placed by the government as an Agent to this people, their advancement in the scale of moral & accountable beings, is to me an object of high importance," he pointed out, "and I know not what could have so direct an influence in raising them to the dignity of life, as the introduction of Christianity." Moreover, Schoolcraft was adamant that attempts either to civilize or assimilate Indians would fail if Christianity did not first replace native religion.

> I am quite satisfied that their *political*, may result from their *moral* motivation. And that all our attempts in the way of agriculture, schooling & the mechanic arts, are liable to miscarry & produce no permanent good, unless their Indian mind can be purified by gospel truth, & cleansed from the besetting sin of a belief in magic, & from idolatry and spirit worship.[4]

Schoolcraft had great hopes for the Ojibwa and believed that natural circumstances made them receptive to Christianity. "No very strong barriers appear to stand in the way of the introduction of Christianity among the northern tribes," he insisted:

> Their institutions, moral and political, are so fragile, as to be ready to tumble on the application of the slightest power. . . . Nothing is

more common, however, in conversing with them, [than] to find individuals, who are ready to acknowledge, the insufficiency of those means, and who appear prepared to abandon them, and embrace the doctrine of the Savior, the moment the fear of popular opinions among *their own people* can be removed.[5]

Yet Schoolcraft's confidence proved far off the mark, as the missionaries whose call to the Upper Great Lakes he engineered quickly discovered. Enthusiasm and hard work notwithstanding, for several decades they made only slight headway. The Christian gospel seemed unable to compete with native religion.

Protestant conversion efforts among the Ojibwa in the United States began with the Moravians, whose history of itinerant evangelism had led them to missionary work earlier than most other churches. Preaching a theology of "blood and wounds" and of the "suffering Savior," their missionaries sought to live humbly among the heathens, to openly exhort the crucified Christ, and to focus on individual conversions.[6] Ojibwa bands first encountered Moravians and converts in chance meetings during the bands' journeys into the Ohio area in the 1770s. What excited Ojibwa interest about Christianity, however, was not the piety of converted Indians, but their prosperity, a fact that subsequently convinced the Moravians that an Ojibwa mission would be inappropriate.[7] Nonetheless, contact increased after 1792, when Rev. David Zeisberger accompanied a group of Christian Delaware Indians to Fairfield, Ontario, in Ojibwa territory. Forced to move several times during the course of the American Revolution, the congregation had petitioned for British asylum and received permission to settle in Fairfield. Once settled, Zeisberger devoted himself exclusively to the Delawares, whom he had shepherded so carefully to safety; his diaries reveal that he made little effort during the first months to bring local Ojibwa into the fold, although he did have occasional meetings and business dealings with them.[8]

It was the Delaware converts themselves who proselytized in the area. "Boaz spoke with a family of Chippewas who came here," Zeisberger recorded in his diary on 10 August 1792, "and extolled to them the salvation which the Savior has won by His blood for all Indians who wish to accept and believe it. He said they had listened attentively."[9] Throughout the autumn months, both Delaware and white Moravians maintained sporadic contact with the Ojibwa but achieved no tangible results. "We have had no increase by outsiders. In the spring, two families came here to live but then left again, and the old ones among them [left in Zeisberger's care] died soon after."[10] By 1795, the minister felt certain that no Ojibwa would convert, for their attachment to traditional beliefs was too strong. "When we once get acquainted with these Indians, we shall see more superstition and heathenism than we have yet seen," he reflected, as the drums of the medicine dance throbbed outside his window.[11]

Finally in 1801, an Ojibwa chief requested a missionary for his community, and Rev. Christian Frederick Denke set up a satellite mission of the Fairfield station at Lake St. Clair. Despite the chief's enthusiasm, however, most of the villagers were immune to Denke's exhortations and deaf to his message; though they were quite obliging about listening to him, they had no intention of apostatizing their own beliefs. Two years after his arrival, Denke abandoned the mission. His subsequent attempt in 1804 to evangelize along the Jonquakamick River proved even less successful, for the local population snubbed any "Sunday Indian" who demonstrated the least interest in Denke's preaching.[12] Tensions escalated when the reverend unwisely took advantage of ritual gatherings and dances to preach the Gospels. He and his wife soon received several death threats, and in September 1806 the Ojibwa initiated a campaign of open harassment against the couple. One individual, according to Denke, "instigated many wicked Chippewas, men, women and children to camp near the mission premises and to indulge in the most heathenish practices, keeping up their shouting, dancing and drumming for several days and nights."[13] Beleaguered by accusations of murder and hounded by the drums, Denke fled the village for Fairfield. But that mission, by now the Moravians' last stand, had also declined by 1808, as the congregants died or emigrated; it finally folded in 1821.

The ABCFM began a similarly abbreviated first attempt in 1823, when William and Amanda Ferry founded a mission and school on Mackinac Island at the tip of Lake Huron. Within the year the Ferrys had attracted thirty young pupils, mostly of mixed blood, to the school, but they found the adults' responses disheartening. Amanda reported to her sister that "we have full meetings and attentive hearers, but they go away not deeply impressed, sauntering about, regardless of the Lord's Day, not knowing what to do. Many on the Island go reeling about, in idleness."[14] Although for a short while she thought that prospects for conversions had picked up, by 1828 few Ojibwa, male or female, had experienced rebirth. Those women who expressed an interest in Christianity generally had strong connections to the white community through blood or marriage. Several traders' wives and their sisters requested religious instruction, as did a desperate woman whose English mother-in-law had removed her children to Britain (where they subsequently died) and who pleaded to join the mission family for comfort in her loss.[15] Only rarely did a native woman without European or American ties seek religious or secular education.[16]

The Ferrys labored on Mackinac Island for eleven years, without leave and with minimal success, until Ferry's resignation in 1834, which was officially attributed to a nervous breakdown. Another missionary's insights, however, suggest that Ferry himself had compromised the mission's status. In 1838, Peter Dougherty, of the Presbyterian Board of Foreign Missions, visited Mackinac en route to his new station at Grand Traverse. Dougherty reported that to all appearances the Ojibwa had not benefited from the Ferrys' efforts among them. "Even the Mission of the A.B. (American Board) can hardly be said to have been one for the Indian," he confided to his diary, "as the most done was to collect some few native children and half breeds into a boarding school. So far as the Indian people are concerned it appears to be doubted whether much good has been affected by the Station here."[17]

His curiosity piqued by the mission's rather mysterious closing, Dougherty investigated the situation in Mackinac, which appeared to him as little more than a tiny village of log huts. He visited Jane Johnson Schoolcraft (a métis married to Indian agent Henry Schoolcraft and granddaughter of the Ojibwa war captain Shin-ga-be-w'ossin), who told a dismal tale of the mission's demise. Ferry had become secularized, she recounted, and business rather than religion became his love. He had other passions as well, which involved young native girls at the mission school. Confronted by the suspicious villagers, Ferry admitted that he had acted imprudently. The Ojibwa parents angrily withdrew their children from the school, and the mission folded with his resignation.[18] If Jane Schoolcraft's account is correct, Ferry's abuse of young girls and his rigid disciplinary code for boys undoubtedly united the entire native community, regardless of gender, against the mission.

In 1829, two traders of the American Fur Company, inspired not by disinterested benevolence but by the hope that Christianity and civilization would make native suppliers more industrious, offered to support ABCFM missionaries at trading posts in the Wisconsin Territory. The board obligingly sent William Boutwell, Sherman Hall, Frederick Ayer, and Edmund Ely to convert the Ojibwa. These four men expeditiously set up operations at La Pointe in 1831 and at Leech Lake, Fond du Lac, and Pokeguma in 1833. With the exception of the La Pointe (Odanah) mission (discussed in chapter 5), the experiences of the ABCFM missionaries followed a pattern similar to those of the Moravians and the Ferrys. Initially, most groups received them with curiosity and some interest. Relations with men were almost uniformly good; those with women varied from amicable to antagonistic. Eventually, however, the missionaries found themselves the objects of escalating hostility, and ultimately they were rejected entirely by the communities they worked among. The cases of William T. Boutwell and Edmund Ely illustrate this pattern well.[19]

When Boutwell opened the Leech Lake station in 1833, a good number of men regularly presented themselves at prayer services. Boutwell's records suggest that virtually all those who attended his services and instruction were men or young men. "Several Indians, among them Old Bizhiki, came to our meeting today," he reported in a typical diary entry. "Three or four of them began to sing. This circumstance encourages me. If they can be enlisted in this way, there is hope, that it will often lead them where they will hear Christian instruction. . . .

Several young men and children came in this evening and joined us in our song, and attended our evening devotions."[20] Sometimes even male shamans attended services, and Sherman Hall reported from La Pointe that one shaman had actually converted.[21]

Like many of his Jesuit predecessors, Boutwell saw native women as drudges, and he generally found their company unpleasant. These prejudices, developed during his travels with Schoolcraft, inevitably carried over into his mission work. In his personal taxonomy, Indians were male: he always distinguished between "Indians and squaws."[22] "Selfishness is a prominent characteristic of the squaws," he sourly observed in one journal entry on the trip out to Wisconsin Territory. "You may give and continue to give, and they are not satisfied. They will eat from morn till night, and still ask for more. An old squaw is one of the most selfish and capricious of beings. . . . The squaws are horribly filthy in their persons, as well as Sluttish in their habits."[23]

Most native ways appalled Boutwell, but women's mannerisms truly repulsed him. During a stopover at Grand Portage in June before arriving at Leech Lake, Boutwell chanced upon a group of women and children casually eating a communal meal in their accustomed fashion. The youngsters, wearing their summer breechclouts, were gathered with the adults, and each plucked morsels from a stew pot, unencumbered by the cutlery that their American counterparts regularly struggled with at meals. The informality of this repast was too much for Boutwell; indeed, his reaction epitomized the cultural gap between his ways and those of the people he intended to save. The ultimate insult to his taste, apparently, was the gusto with which one woman meticulously polished off the remainder of the meal. "There I saw more of the habits of Indian neatness. To see them eat," he declared,

> is enough to disgust forever even a hungry man. All get around the kettle, or soup dish, and each uses his fingers or the whole hand, even, to the best advantage. Children, entirely naked, except a strip of cloth two inches in width, tied in a knot before, and which served for a breech-cloth, these I could endure, but to see a squaw lick a kettle cover, both in diamater and circumference, is a little too much.[24]

Without doubt, most of the young ladies of Boutwell's acquaintance, practitioners of the womanly domestic arts of the nineteenth-century middle class, were far daintier in their mannerisms. What Boutwell did not comprehend, however, was that they also were not faced annually with the specter of winter starvation, which had prompted Ojibwa to develop a cultural pattern of eating copiously when food was available.

Boutwell's dreary opinion of women extended beyond the realm of the gastronomical. Like Jesuits and Wesleyans, he also avoided women to protect his reputation: "I am obliged to be very careful, and practice much reserve in visiting the lodges as the men are mostly absent, lest I should give occasion for evil speaking, and lay myself open to slander."[25] But Boutwell's delicacy far exceeded the demands of protocol. His contempt for women was palpable, as his report of New Year festivities made clear:

> An old squaw, with clean face, for once, came up and saluted me with "bon jour," giving her hand at the same time, which I recieved, returning her compliment, "bon jour." But this was not all. She had been too long among Canadians not to learn some of their New Year customs. She approached—approached so near, to give and recieve a kiss, that I was obliged to give her a slip, and dodge! This vexed the old lady and provoked her to say, that I thought her too dirty.

The woman's wounded pride, however, did not deter him. "Pleased, or displeased, I was determined to give no countenance to a custom which I hated more than dirt. . . . The young women, seeing the rebuff of the old lady, were not a little ashamed, apparently, and kept their proper and becoming distance."[26]

Obviously, Boutwell's attitude was not going to endear him to women. Unfortunately, the problematic relationship between the minister and the Ojibwa women of Leech Lake went beyond Boutwell's Anglo-American criteria for comeliness and propriety. Not only was he offensive and uncompromising in his rejection of native ways, but his religious message was apparently seen as threatening and prompted women to mistrust his intentions in settling among them. For more than a year most of the women refused to participate in his services; only in January

1834 did Boutwell manage to get some involved at all. "Not until this evening, have I been able to get the females to make an attempt to sing," he confessed in his diary. "As I was alone with the little boys who sing, I determined they should make an effort to conquer their fears, or rather their pride. It was not without a little resolution and perseverance that I prevailed on them."[27] Furthermore, the women's daughters also resolutely avoided the missionary. "A little girl came in [to school], whom I asked the question if she would like to learn to read. No, replied she. Whether it is fear or shame, I cannot tell, that keeps the little girls from wishing to learn," Boutwell mused.[28]

Although it did not occur to Boutwell, unfamiliar as he was with local custom, it may be that women actually discouraged girls from attending classes. School attendance took a girl away from her mother during the crucial time leading up to puberty. In the years before adolescence, from age four or five on, children fasted for visions, seeking spiritual power from supernaturals or animal spirits. Little girls, their faces blackened with charcoal, went into the woods alone for the day without food or drink in hope of talking to the spirits. Older girls stayed four or more days in the bush, fasting, sleeping, and dreaming while seeking the powers of medicine women or the tutelage of animal supernaturals. On her return home, a child received a ritual welcome and feast from her mother or another female relative, after which she recounted the guardian-spirit dreams of her fasting time.[29]

At first menstruation, girls retired in isolation for four to ten days in special small wigwams constructed by the girls or their mothers and grandmothers near the home lodge. During this time a girl was extremely potent spiritually, and it was imperative that she remain apart to avoid overriding men's hunting powers or infants' weak spirits. This was her initiation into womanhood, when her mother instructed her in new responsibilities and how to be a good person. Because idleness was prohibited, she was required to sew or do beadwork throughout the day. After a daughter's seclusion had ended and she was welcomed back into the family with a feast, her grandmother or a female relative supervised her constantly until marriage.[30] Consequently, if a girl attended daily school or lived at a boarding school, her mother would be unable to arrange her prepuberty fasting or menstrual seclusion; in any case, missionaries were hardly receptive to a girl following such non-Christian rituals.

Women resisted Boutwell's efforts to incorporate them into mission life and continued on with customary practices. In August 1833, Boutwell made inquiries about a Grand Medicine Dance (Midewiwin) lodge recently constructed near the mission and found that "this dance . . . was made for the purpose of initiating one or two old squaws into some of the higher mysteries of their grand medicine, for which they must pay a handsome fee."[31] The Leech Lake women even absorbed the childbirth of the local post trader's wife, Mrs. Davenport, into their ritual world. Boutwell reported that "the ignorant and superstitious old women" berated the trader for treating her poorly and blamed her long travail on his selfish behavior. They set all hostilities aside following the infant's birth, however, to celebrate. Boutwell recorded the event:

> The old squaws this morning collected in the lodge, and made a feast, which I am told is customary after a birth. It consisted of sugar only, I am informed. At its commencement, one of their number made a long harangue, which, from the few words I could understand, seemed a kind of address to the Great and Good, but unknown God, in behalf of the child. The same address concluded the feast, without which they could not put aside their potent medicine sacks.[32]

The women's insistence on observing birthing rituals, even for a white woman, seems a powerful testimony to the continued importance of tradition in their lives. Birth rites, in their very femaleness, reflected women's faith in the vitality of native traditions and the importance of their own roles in sustaining them.

In addition to persisting in their observance of rituals, a few women openly opposed Boutwell. During his first year, Boutwell and Sherman Hall, a fellow ABCFM missionary visiting from Chequamegon, called on a family whose young son had just died of illness. The ministers hoped to perform a Christian burial, but when they asked permission of the group's leader, the man appeared reluctant to answer. The boy's mother, however, unhesitatingly refused. "After we returned," Boutwell explained,

> we learned that the old squaw, the mother of the deceased, said when Mr. H[all] visited them in the morning, that we might assist in burying so far as the grave, coffin & c. were concerned, but that she would have none of our singing or praying. We learned also that this old squaw, a few days before, brought her son from Montreal River, 21 miles from this, that the Indians might make a medicine dance on his account.[33]

Boutwell recorded a similar incident several years later. In March 1836, he administered a cathartic to a sick boy at the grandmother's request; the child died the following day and, upon the father's wishes, received the first Christian burial in the area. Later the child's grandparents argued over Boutwell's responsibility for the death. The grandmother pointedly remarked, "The Indians say that they are sick, because the blackcoat is here, and it was not so before he came." Her husband, one of Boutwell's supporters, scoffed and insisted, "The Indians are fools, and those very persons who say such things are the ones who come to him for medicines."[34] This couple's difference of opinion reflects a general pattern of response among Ojibwa communities: the grandfather, like other men, found Boutwell's program at the mission compelling, while the grandmother remained unconvinced.

On an individual level, the case of Memengua, although admittedly inconclusive, suggests that women's opposition to Boutwell carried weight in the Leech Lake communities. Memengua had asked Boutwell to keep his eldest son for instruction over the winter of 1833–34. Delighted, Boutwell agreed to take the boy until the mother's consent had been obtained. Within two weeks of the father's departure, however, Boutwell received orders from Memengua "not to learn him [the son] prayers, in either English, French, or Indian."[35] Boutwell never explained why the plan failed. It may well be that Memengua's wife objected to the boy's involvement with the missionary.

The gulf between Boutwell and the women of Leech Lake widened as a result of the young minister's callous self-interest during crisis, with ramifications for the entire community. In early March 1834, the women and children made their yearly trek to the maple groves to tap trees while the men went off to hunt. Boutwell stayed at the mission and planned regular trips to the sugar camps to instruct the children as the women collected, boiled, and evaporated the sap. Sugaring was one of the most enjoyable events of the year; everyone usually relished the fun and good foods retrieved from caches near the sugar camps. But this spring was a fickle one, and a deadly cold settled over the region. "For 10 days the weather has been so cold, as to freeze up everything, and stop all operations in the sugar camps. The Indian women and children are now, and have for several days, been in a starving condition, having spent all their corn, rice and the little sugar they made during the mild weather at the opening of the month."[36] With each day the situation grew more desperate, and even the Boutwells found themselves reduced to eating boiled cornmeal and deer tallow. This must have seemed a feast, however, to the starving Ojibwa mothers, desperate to get any scraps they could for their families. "The meager and haggard physiognomy of the women and children, as well as their scraping our pudding kettle with their fingers when they come in, bespeaks hunger, indeed," Boutwell noted.[37] Several days later the missionary again complained of the tedious diet of mush and salt, but thanked Providence that his family could eat even as Indians starved all around them.[38] To the Ojibwa, Boutwell's uncharitable behavior in hoarding his food rather than sharing must have been incomprehensible. In native society the welfare and survival of the community was paramount; individual greed could not threaten the society as a whole. The missionary's refusal to open his provisions flouted Ojibwa morals and betrayed his emotional distance from the people.

After several years, entire communities became suspicious of the missionary and impatient with his attitude. Boutwell's blundering self-centeredness helped solidify the opposition, and by 1836 he had antagonized all the bands around Leech Lake. That October, a throng of men surrounded his home, threatened to kill his cattle, and accused him of revealing Ojibwa war plans to a U.S. government agency. Boutwell only narrowly avoided a fiasco by plying them with foodstuffs. They minced no words, however, when advising him that he stand with them, and they rebuked him for his parsimony and arrogance. "And now I will give you a few hints how you must do," Black Bird announced, "if you stay here this winter":

> You must never say anything to our children or young men if they strike or injure your cattle, not even to the youngest, for they will tell of it—if they dont their companions will. And should you make another garden, and they should steal from it, you must not reprove them or say anything to them. But if you will not go away next summer, we will warn you before-hand that we are stronger than one man, we will all of us come together, and put you in a canoe and shove you off. . . . You dont do us any good, at all, by being here, but the traders bring us goods, and therefore the Indians are determined that you shall not stay another year.[39]

Boutwell remained at the station through the next year but understandably grew increasingly depressed about his situation. Ojibwa hostility (and the tightened purse strings of the ABCFM) finally forced him to close the mission in late 1837.[40] Some years later, upon his final resignation, Boutwell reflected on his reasons for leaving the board:

> It is not that I am weary of my work among this benighted & degraded people. No, I am as ready to live & labor for God among them as ever, could I but see the finger of his Providence directing to a spot where in our judgement we could do them good. Indeed I should not dare to leave this field, did I see or feel that God had anything further for me to do for them. They have seen the light but hate & reject it—In the language of a drunken pagan to bro. H. [Hall] when here a few days since—"You have the Book & Know God, you will stand at the right hand, but I am wicked & I shall stand at the left hand."[41]

Clearly Boutwell never was able to comprehend Ojibwa values or the tenacity of their beliefs.

The experiences of Edmund Franklin Ely, a teacher and another of the ABCFM missionaries to the Ojibwa, ran close to Boutwell's. Although exotic native ways immediately impressed Ely, as they had Boutwell, he responded with less hostility and,

indeed, some humility. The rhythm and power of Ojibwa dancing and drumming awed him. "The air was singing with the
sound of their drums—their songs and yells," he reported in
August 1833, after his arrival at Fond du Lac, an important
center of tribal activities and a trading post 120 miles from La
Pointe. While not sympathetic to traditional beliefs—he found
the Midewiwin induction ceremony observed by Boutwell to be
"quite a ridiculous farce"—Ojibwa language and culture nonetheless intrigued him, and he relished his dealings with the
young men with whom he had daily instruction.[42]

Initially, Ely found himself and the new mission well received
by men and women alike. Within the month, one man, Brusia,
had asked Ely to teach his sons to read and write; as for himself,
he "wished to learn to sing." People came and went at Ely's
lodgings all day, to chat and join in singing or simply to pass the
time visiting quietly. By late September he had begun to instruct the children, though their attendance was somewhat
irregular.[43] Parents allowed their daughters to attend both day
and evening schools. Youngsters frequently appeared at his
door after supper eager to sing and listen to scriptural
readings.[44] Ely spent long and happy hours with the children,
singing, looking at scriptural engravings, discussing hymns,
and practicing spelling, until he concluded the evening with a
prayer. Moreover, unlike Boutwell, Ely apparently neither
frightened nor offended the women. In fact, several attended
weekly services, and they particularly enjoyed singing.[45]

Despite this apparent success, Ely wallowed in self-doubt
during this time. He felt only "an amazing apathy" toward his
Savior, and was convinced that he and the mission were dismal
failures.

> I never so much saw my deficiencies as at this time. I seem to lack
> the important requisites of a successful missionary—spirituality—
> meekness—love—humility—& I know that Christ can alone de-
> liver. I believe, that Satan tried to throw discouragement before my
> mind yesterday. [Mr. Davenport] began to tell me of the remarks &
> laughings of the Indians with regard to our coming here—& added
> that until civilization took place among them, our labours were in
> vain & offered to lay a *bet* with me that one convert would not be
> added to us in ten Years to come.[46]

Ely's spirits plummeted still further when informed by Mr. Cottee (Coté), a post trader who had been instructing Ojibwa in Catholicism, that "some of the Men had cut their Hair—& broken their Drums—thereby renouncing paganism & embracing Catholicism."[47] Although women had attended his Sabbath services regularly, Ely believed that without the men he was making little headway. His problems were exacerbated in early October 1834, he reported, by the arrival of a group of Ojibwa to trade for ammunition. One of the newcomers begged the Fond du Lac people not to become praying Indians and warned them of the dreadful impact conversion would have on them:

> He said that, "last fall, the *Stars* fell—so the Indians would eventually fall before the Americans if they became praying Indians." He added a remarkable vision, wh[ic]h took place this Summer—in the Folle Avoigne. Nine Canoes happened to meet in a River on the same night—flambeauing for deer—(18 *men*) *Nanibosho* appeared to them by a Voice in the heavens—saying—"*Kiji-Anomiakegon*."[48]

Ely's outlook improved remarkably, however, after several men began attending classes at the end of the month. One middle-aged man expressed a desire to know the Book—and three or four were real scholars. Ely soon happily observed that requests for instruction were becoming more frequent, that the men enjoyed watching him write, and that they were, in fact, quite kind.[49] From this point, Ely's journal entries often emphasized the number of men attending classes or requesting additional instruction. The men's interest in literacy continued to increase, and they soon asked for evening classes in geography and the "cause of day & night."[50] They generally brought their sons with them for lessons. Ely observed in the early winter of 1835 that the older men strongly favored education and fervently wished that "they could read the Book."[51]

During the same period, though, he also reported that parents complained that their children were "growing ungovernable at home and at school under my government and instruction." One girl even hurled epithets at him in class. Corporal punishment in the classroom had infuriated the children, he discovered, and the parents felt that my *pulling the Hair of the Children* was a cruel & degrading punishment—& calculated to make the scholars very angry. . . . [Mr. Cottee] said the children told him that I pulled out much of their hair—so that it lay about the floor. (In one or two instances, when a child shrank from my grasp—& I not willing to release, until they submitted a few Hairs—(& a very few)—have been taken out) I inquired if the Indians felt it peculiarly degrading to be taken by the Hair? He ans[were]d Yes!—I plead ignorance of the fact—& expressed a willingness to dispense with this kind of punishment.[52]

The children may have been more aggrieved by Ely's discipline than were their parents, but his lack of diplomacy undoubtedly undermined his efforts. Corporal punishment, when used at all by Ojibwa parents, was generally limited to light spankings with slender sticks on hand or knees and was reserved for more serious offenses. More often, a mother might scold a recalcitrant child or threaten that an owl would come and take her or him away.[53]

Slowly, Ely's audience became almost exclusively male, though he still made mention in his journals of one or two girls in school and an occasional woman at services. His female pupils and congregants seemed to fade away, a fact that he noticed but did not find disturbing. "Services as usual," he reported in May 1835. "Immediately after Service, my house was thronged with men (Catholics mostly) (Inds). They requested to hear Christs death, & also—where C commands to *watch & pray*—which I read to them." And the following month he remarked, "My lodge was pretty well filled at the Children's meeting this P.M. Nearly 40, men & children were present."[54]

In late May, Ely and the other ABCFM missionaries gathered at the La Pointe mission for the summer. There he met two recent converts, Henry Blatchford and Catherine Galois Bissell, mixed-bloods educated at the Ferrys' old Mackinac mission and now hired as assistants for La Pointe. Evidently taken with Bissell, Ely married her in late August. In September, the missionaries decided to close the Fond du Lac station and have the Elys remain at La Pointe. While there, the couple did attempt to reach the local women, and felt quite pleased with their small success.[55]

This Evening, by invitation, 5 or 6 Indian women came to my room, expressly to learn to Knit. We sung some Hymns. I read, the story of C. walking on the sea & concluded with prayer. All appeared highly gratified. After they had retired, we united in Thanksgiving to God for inclining The hearts of those women to come among us—& listen to His word. May God bring good out of this.[56]

However, the Elys did not have time to continue their work with the women of La Pointe, as the missionaries rather suddenly reversed their decision about Fond du Lac a few weeks later.[57]

Back at the station at the end of October, Ely resumed his work with the men. Most of the younger males, including sons of the chief Ma-osit, came regularly for scriptural readings and evening worship. They listened attentively, with an easy camaraderie, as Ely earnestly explained to them that there was one God, one Bible, and that Christ came to save them all; "Mamokotakomik [wonderful]," one fellow repeatedly rejoined.[58] Stirred by Ely's prayers and exhortations, men like Kashkibazh, Ininini, and Shinguabe soon reflected on the evils of their lives before they had come to know Christ.[59]

Guakuekegabau stood out among the neophytes for the burning intensity with which he pursued his new religion. Disconcerted by the man's fervor, Ely suspiciously queried him about his true motivation for converting. What could he say when Guakuekegabau responded that "he wanted a new heart. He wanted the spirit of God to sanctify him." Still cautious, the missionary pursued the issue and to his delight found that Guakuekegabau indeed had burned his medicine bundle and his drums and renounced all other gods. Even Ma-osit, "one of the 'Mighty Medicine Men,'" gave up "his Mitiguokik—Medicine Sack & Rattle—to the missionaries."[60] Success seemed at hand.

Like Boutwell, Ely had come to see the men as "the Indians"; native women began to appear in his journal as ancillary figures, adornments to the male. He never referred to women by name, only by their relationship to a man. From their near absence in his later notes, it seems that Ely gave up on the women, or perhaps they simply withdrew from mission activities as their initial curiosity about Ely diminished and his lack of interest in them became clear. The case of Ma-osit's wife suggests that what interest there was among women came, once again, at their husbands' demand. When the shaman Ma-osit converted, Ely commented that although the wife had also embraced Christianity, he was certain her commitment was only nominal. She confirmed his suspicions when Catherine Ely caught her defiantly and unrepentantly breaking the Sabbath to sew.[61] Likewise, when Baiejik, who by 1840 had been under Ely's tutelage for three years, requested not only his own baptism but that of his entire family as well, Ely interviewed his spouse that February. She informed him that she could not give up her old habits and therefore assumed that she had no real hope of salvation. Two years later, when Ely finally baptized Baiejik and the children, she was noticeably absent.[62]

To be sure, not all men greeted Ely's efforts with enthusiasm, and many who initially did later changed their minds. Edninabondo branded any Ojibwa who sought an education a fool, since "God had made the white men for such knowledge." Ely, apparently unaware of the larger issues at hand, insisted that Indians were as capable as anyone else and pressed the man to explain further. Edninabondo retorted "that since the american teachers had come among them, the Indians had begun to die, &c."[63] Others claimed, with some perspicacity, that Ely was really the forerunner of settlers who wanted to drive Ojibwa off their lands. Some especially suspicious critics fiercely maintained that Ely and all missionaries were in fact agents of the U.S. government sent to enslave them.[64]

Again like Boutwell, Ely eventually found himself the object of mounting hostility. By the summer of 1838 conflict swirled through the community, centered on the issue of some land for which he had contracted to plant crops and graze cattle. Angry and disconcerted, the missionary anxiously observed that "scarce a day passes but the Indians show their hatred or opposition to us,—in words concerning our residence here—the land—wood—grass—fish—that we use—& from all that we can judge, it is evident they intend to take some oppressive course with us." He complained bitterly when the Ojibwa shot one of his cattle in the leg. "O! It is trying—trying—to live &

deal with such a people."[65] They, in return, insisted that Ely's proprietary attitude toward the land was selfish.

The situation exploded in August. While Ely cut hay one afternoon, a crowd killed and skinned his bull, then had the audacity to butcher it in front of him upon his return home. He furiously confronted them, but "they manifested no regret. On the other hand they told me if I felt sad about it, the best way was for me to leave the Country—that I might not be sad again—for perhaps They might do something worse."[66] Ely took the warning to heart: by the following year he had joined William Boutwell and Frederick Ayer at the Pokeguma mission, which itself would be destroyed by Dakota raids within a few years.[67] All in all, the missionaries had found that the natives whom they expected to convert easily had at best a mixed response.

Other factors, of course, influenced the survival of the missions. The evangelists' inadequate preparation, inability to speak the language, personal and family concerns, and ignorance of native social organization contributed to the problems they faced. Interdenominational hostility played a role as well; French Catholics at Mackinac were in an uproar when the Ferrys established their mission. "They soon secured a Priest," Amanda reported to a friend, "erected a church and are unwearied in their efforts to 'root out' the 'heretics' from all their borders."[68] To the Ferrys' indignation, the priest forbade Indians from attending Protestant instruction. It appears to have been a hollow gesture: Dougherty commented cynically in 1838 that the Catholics had done nothing for the Indians either.

German Lutherans at Frankenmuth farther south in Michigan found themselves at odds with itinerant Methodists, who attempted to keep the Ojibwa from sending their children to the Lutheran school by spreading rumors that Lutheran converts would be sent to England as slaves. These efforts backfired, however. The converted chief Bemassikeh scornfully berated the Methodists for both their aggressive approach and their manner of worship. As he described the confrontation,

> The German [Lutheran] blackcoat visited me first; we are friends and wish to remain such. But you I do not like. You howl early and

late, and leap and move hands and legs as if you would jump into heaven. When a short time ago my son died, I also lamented, for he was my son. But you howl without cause, until God shall give you a cause; then indeed you may howl.[69]

As in the Hudson Bay Territory, Ojibwa reactions to early-nineteenth-century missions in the United States evinced little of the gender differential so apparent in the Jesuit era. These missionaries did not challenge women's self-interest as females. Whatever initial curiosity women might have had about Christianity withered from lack of attention, a development that defused most situations conducive to gender-based resistance. Unlike most Ojibwa and Cree in Canada, however, in the Great Lakes area whole communities came to perceive missionaries as threats, as agents of change and destruction, and demanded their departure. Only later, when white settlement threatened to overwhelm them and many native men began to view missionaries as useful allies, did women once again openly confront missionaries and defend their interests as females.

□ 5 □
THE FIRST PATTERN REPEATED
"The Trouble Is with the Women"

Although most Ojibwa communities did not threaten to shove missionaries downriver, many clearly considered the clergy a menace to collective security and cultural integrity. Despite this attitude, however, some missions did endure, if not thrive. While their survival certainly reflected clerical tenacity, more importantly it indicated the political and economic exigencies faced by local native populations. During the period 1830–1870, Ojibwa experienced mounting pressure from white encroachment into the northern forests of Michigan, Wisconsin, and Minnesota. Wisconsin Ojibwa ceded all their lands to the United States, and those in Minnesota and Michigan relinquished land or mineral rights for much of their territories. Throughout the 1850s and 1860s, too, the federal government attempted to relocate Ojibwa to small, isolated reservations throughout the three states.[1]

A community's vulnerability to these circumstances varied with its proximity to mineral deposits, timber stands, or white settlements—and so did its receptivity to proselytization. Although more isolated groups resisted conversion efforts throughout the nineteenth century, under the pressure of contact others were compelled to allow evangelists to work among them. Mission stations such as the two that are the subject of this chapter, Odanah (La Pointe, Wisconsin) and Omena (Grand Traverse, Michigan), were adjacent to focal points for relocation and resource development and held out the possibility of education and Christianity as final defenses against annihilation. As the missionary Sherman Hall wrote to his brother from La Pointe in 1845, "I believe christianity is the only remedy for their present wretched condition. And this is an adequate remedy, if they would embrace it with all the heart, and become true followers of Christ."[2] His successor, Leonard Wheeler, repeated this warning seven years later: "The last experiment is now being tried, which is to decide the question whether the Indians are to be civilized, christianized, and constitute a part of the permanent inhabitants of our country or whether they are to be left . . . to those wasting influences which threaten their destruction."[3] It is in communities that heeded this caveat and allowed mission stations to remain among them that a gender-specific response to Christianity and colonization reappeared.

Frederick Ayer opened the first mission at La Pointe in 1830, following a request by American Fur Company traders that the American Board of Commissioners of Foreign Missions establish stations in Wisconsin Territory. Sherman Hall and William Boutwell arrived the following year, fresh from their ordinations at Andover Seminary. Hall remained at La Pointe for the next twenty years, while Boutwell, Ayer, Ely, and others dispersed to Leech Lake and other satellite sites at Yellow Lake, Pokeguma, Fond du Lac, and Sandy Lake.[4]

Hall had fifteen to twenty students when he began teaching in 1832, but he soon became convinced that neither Christianity nor fear of final judgment impressed the Ojibwa. It would, he concluded, be a long process to raise the natives up.[5] At times during that year he thought that perhaps the adults' "prejudices and fears" had decreased and they soon would happily send their children for instruction, but at other moments he had to admit that "we are ba[r]barians to the Indians and they to us."[6] Yet by the next year, even though it was clear that "heathenism is heathenism still," a number of young men and women had expressed an interest in learning to read, the missionaries had compiled an Ojibwa spelling book, and Hall felt comfortable recommending to the ABCFM that the station open a boarding school.[7]

Over the next few years the mission slowly but steadily expanded. A number of Ojibwa families settled in permanent homes, and the school was relatively well attended, if not quite a model classroom. "I wish you could just take a look into it," Hall wrote to his sister in Vermont, "and see the little, ragged, dirty, lousy and disgusting little objects trying to learn to read their own language and write on slates. Though they are filthy, it is a pleasure to teach them the word of life, which they can also teach their parents."[8] He thought it unfortunate that so many students were mixed-bloods, but like other missionaries, he found that the majority of full-blood Ojibwa were quite indifferent to religious instruction. Despite this barrier, Hall felt sure that their prejudices against him were weakening and that he was gaining on his Catholic competitors.[9] Roman Catholics also had been at La Pointe since Rev. Frederic Baraga's visits in 1835, but despite an initial rash of native conversions, St. Joseph's served a primarily mixed-blood parish and baptized few Ojibwa after 1840.[10]

It was not until the events of 1842–43, however, that Hall saw any significant change in native attitudes. This followed the La Pointe treaty of October 1842, in which the Ojibwa ceded mineral rights to much of their lands, on which whites had discovered copper in 1840.[11] Part of the compact specified that $1,500 be paid to the ABCFM schools for 1842 and the first six months of 1843. The treaty was a coup for the United States: it opened up copper and iron lands, initiated a series of land surveys in the area, and established a federal Mineral Land Agency office.

Between three and four thousand Ojibwa, weakened and vulnerable from a grim winter of starvation so severe that families went without food for days, met with Commissioner of Indian Affairs Robert Stuart in 1843 to continue treaty negotiations and clarify specific payment amounts.[12] The commissioner, taking advantage of his literally captive audience, harangued them on the virtues of Christianity:

> [You] Indians remain poor & ignorant. But if you will educate your children, they will become as rich & as wise as the whites. They will also learn to worship the Great Spirit aright. I hope you will open your ears and hearts to receive this free advice and then you will get great Sight. But I am afraid of [for] you, because though your missionaries preach here every night, you do not come. They are anxious you should hear the word of God and be wise and have peace among yourselves.[13]

Along with the advice, Stuart offered annuities in money, goods, and provisions for twenty-five years, plus a yearly school allowance: $12,000 in cash, $10,000 in goods, $2,000 in provisions and tobacco, and $2,000 for the school.[14]

In the ensuing years, Hall and the mission teacher, Leonard Wheeler, reported that many more Ojibwa than ever before seemed unsure of their traditional practices and inclined to receive religious instruction. Prayer meetings at outlying stations now resulted in the conversions of several important men. The convert Martin Luther exemplified the distress of those who felt the efficacy of their beliefs had waned; "I believe . . . in the great Spirit of the bible—that he is the true God, for I see every thing he has made around me—But where are our Gods? we cannot find a track of them—we called any thing a *manito* (spirit)—I have tried all our gods and know that there is nothing in our religion."[15] By 1847, Hall had convinced a number of Ojibwa that Christianity and sedentary farming were their only protection against the impact of immigration. Smallpox epidemics and the influx of white settlers, drawn by the potential for mining and lumber into competition for native territory, capped his argument.[16] Hall reported to his sister that, with speculators buying up land and introducing whiskey, "[the Ojibwa] are in a state of peril. White immigration is rolling in upon them like a flood. Portions of the country they now occupy are wanted."[17]

During 1846–47, the ABCFM opened the Odanah satellite station, on what was to become the Bad River reservation. After scouting the area in 1845, Leonard Wheeler had decided that it was the best site for a school, especially since the federal government intended to relocate the La Pointe Ojibwa there. Initially, the local inhabitants' response was poor; although most welcomed Wheeler, few attended services for fear of community ridicule.[18] Within the decade, however, this situation would change as the government escalated pressure on Wisconsin Ojibwa to relocate west of the Mississippi. The original plans called for removal of the La Pointe groups during the summer of 1851; most groups refused to move, though, and the missionaries were certain the relocation would take place only with force. At this point, Wheeler played his hand. Meeting with chiefs and headmen, he announced that survival rested on their ability to adopt the habits of whites—to cultivate the soil, educate their children, and embrace white religion. After discussing in council the merits of changing religions, the men agreed to Wheeler's strategy.

Wheeler was sharp enough to recognize that this metamorphosis came from the men's dissatisfaction with the apparent failure of native rituals rather than a sudden infusion of grace, and from the realization that in order to remain at Bad River they must attend meetings and send their offspring to school.[19] Although Odanah was not besieged immediately with prospective converts, its situation soon improved and attendance at prayer meetings and school increased. This change heartened Wheeler. "It is interesting to see what a beam of intelligence sparkles in the eyes of such children," he remarked, "compared with the vacant stare of the wild untaught Indian child."[20]

In 1853, the board closed the floundering La Pointe mission and sold it to a fishing business. Attendance at meetings and school had dropped over the preceding years as the pressures of white settlement and impending removal loomed ever larger. Sherman Hall moved on to the Crow Wing Agency in Minnesota, where he assumed the position of superintendent of the government manual labor school and opened a new ABCFM mission. He remained there until 1855, when the board closed the station owing to lack of interest from local Indians.[21]

Meanwhile at Odanah, now the last ABCFM mission to the Wisconsin Ojibwa, Wheeler could boast that only one Midewiwin ceremony had been held. The mission's position seemed to be secured when the treaty of 1854 provided the Ojibwa with three reservations in Wisconsin, including Bad River, in return for their part in the cession of six million acres to the federal government; the Odanah mission was included in this agreement. A report from the local Indian agent to the commissioner of Indian affairs indicated that approximately one thousand Ojibwa lived around the Odanah mission, and another fifteen hundred would be moving in from the Lac du Flambeau and Lac Court Oreilles areas.[22] Within the year, several chiefs and others identified themselves as Christians, more chiefs "renounced paganism and joined the christian party," and Wheeler soon reported that while converts were still in the minority, meetings were popular and baptisms continued.[23] A good many made it known that "they had pretty much made up their minds to abandon paganism & adopt the religion & ways of the white man, and proposed to sign a paper to that effect. . . . Worldly policy is mixed up with this to a certain extent," Wheeler admitted, "but they evinced a degree of sincerity upon the subject that I have never before seen."[24]

Ojibwa desire for education continued to increase, and in 1859 Wheeler opened a manual labor boarding school; within two years it had twenty-four students enrolled and a waiting list.[25] There was some disagreement between Wheeler and the lay teachers about how successful the school was. Some teachers claimed that most Ojibwa parents were not ready to relinquish their children to the school. Where Wheeler saw success, some saw crowded conditions. "I ought, perhaps, to remark something of the effects of crowding from 40 to 70 dirty vicious Indian children in so poor a schoolhouse,—both on the teacher & scholars, but I forbear," wrote A. P. Truesdell to ABCFM headquarters, " . . . for, as my wife says, no one, but ourselves, knows how much I have suffered from the poisonous atmosphere of that wretched school room & its inmates."[26] Wheeler, however, was delighted by the growing individualism evident in the natives' desire for private plots of land and in the young men's interest in wage labor at the mission or with local mining, lumber, and fishing companies. A labor shortage created in the mining areas by the Civil War further stimulated this preoccupation.[27]

> We observe with pleasure a decided increase of individual enterprise among them. There is no waiting, as formerly, for another as though afraid to step outside the beaten track their fathers had trod before them. Each man expects to labor personally for the support of himself & family, casting about with Yankee sagacity to see how he can best attain these ends, without waiting to see what his neighbor will think of his conduct. The consequence is more individual independence—more personal industry & thrift; and a greater distinction among them.[28]

In the end, however, political and economic factors once again disturbed the equilibrium of both the Ojibwa and the mission. White hostility against Indians around the Great Lakes escalated following the Little Crow War in Minnesota in 1862, when Dakota warriors killed twenty whites and captured ten. Moreover, Wheeler found many Ojibwa disaffected by the combination of the government's failure to issue land patents, the reassignment of the Bad River reserve from the Michigan Indian agency to a local agent, and fraudulent payment arrangements. The Bad River Ojibwa were transferred to Bayfield in a manipulative deal involving money and whiskey, in which several chiefs signed over part of the payment from the 1854 treaty to property traders, among them a Senator Bright. Although the Bad River reservation incorporated five townships, the agency—which housed the only mill and physician—was located in Bayfield, twenty miles from Odanah, the largest Indian settlement.[29] As Wheeler reported,

> They have been disturbed too by fears of a removal and various have conspired to produce in their minds a general distrust of the whites and a disposition on the part of many to go back to their old pagan habits. A majority of the Indians have planted less this spring than usual, and have manifested little desire for improvement. Feasting—dancing—drumming & ballplaying, have engrossed most of their attentions.[30]

In 1865, Wheeler proposed that the boarding school be closed despite its ongoing popularity, as the facility had become too expensive to maintain after copper prices dropped in the wake of the Civil War. Many Ojibwa regretted both Wheeler's departure and the closing of the manual labor school the next year and requested that the day school continue to operate. The mission and the Ojibwa struggled along. Henry Blatchford, Wheeler's replacement, reported that non-Christians remained "wedded to their idols & superstitions," while the "heathen party" clung to its beliefs but seemed *"less heathen."*[31] In 1870, the ABCFM decided to relinquish Odanah to the Presbyterian Board of Foreign Missions (BFM).[32]

The BFM was the conservative offspring of the 1837 schism between the Old and New schools of the Presbyterian church, a split precipitated by conflict over interdenominational mission societies such as the American Board of Commissioners of Foreign Missions. The Old School, clinging to a defined theology and church authority, rebelled against the ecumenical approach of the ABCFM; following the rupture, Old School Presbyterians created the Board of Foreign Missions from the remains of the Pittsburgh Western Foreign Missionary Society.[33] The BFM saw education as the key to inducing natives to reject tradition and embrace the gospel. Its missionaries were sure that if they could transform the characters of Indian children, native culture would perish and each Indian would become an assimilated citizen. Day and boarding schools therefore were central concerns of both the Odanah and the Omena missions.

The Odanah mission was taken over by the BFM in 1872, when the ABCFM turned control of all its missions over to the now reunited Presbyterian church, and it survived another fourteen years. Men continued to make up the bulk of the converts. Following the first camp meeting in 1878—which lasted a week and was "a little wild and incoherent"—five young men decided to become missionaries to the surrounding reserves. Incidents recorded subsequently suggest that the combination of Christianity and education increasingly attracted men as the perimeters of the native world tightened: railroad lines crossed the reserves, dividing bands, and many men were forced to work for white-owned lumber companies to survive.[34] Of the eleven converts from the period 1883–85, all but two were men.

While the majority of recorded converts under the ABCFM were male, women apparently did not openly oppose the church or school, but neither were they very interested. At E. R. Baierlein's German Lutheran mission to the Ojibwa along the Saginaw River (established at the request of Bemassikeh, a local chief impressed by the Lutherans' nearby colony of Frankenmuth), children were required to attend school and everyone worshiped on Sunday. Baierlein found, however, that while the men listened to his sermons, the women ignored him, chatting loudly with one another and shouting reprimands to their children.[35] At Odanah only limited attempts were made to involve women in mission activities, although Wheeler did conduct weekly female prayer meetings and monthly mothers' meetings, both of which he considered fairly successful.[36] Girls attended the day and boarding schools, but the missionaries did not usually place particular stress on their participation.

This situation changed with the 1876 arrival of Isaac Baird, BFM supervisor of the main station and satellite missions at Round Lake, Lac du Flambeau, Lac Court Oreilles, and Pahquayahwang. Baird insisted on female education, and he emphasized its importance in a report to the BFM: "The girls will need the training more than the boys & they will wield a greater influence in the future. *If we get the girls, we get the race*" (my emphasis).[37] Women shaped the rising generation, he contended, and the missions would succeed only with female support. Soon after his arrival, Baird optimistically informed BFM secretary John C. Lowrie that the school had an "excess" of female students for the first time. The situation was short-lived, however, for over the next ten years male students consistently outnumbered female. The continuing shortfall of mission girls was not for lack of effort on Baird's part; rather, he attributed the girls' absence from school to several cultural factors. "The idea prevalent among heathen Indians is, that it may be well enough to educate the boys somewhat, but as the only future before a girl is a life of menial servitude, she does not need education"—an explanation reflective of his own perceptions of native women's roles.[38] Baird also commented to the local U.S. Indian agent that the amount of time girls spent with their mothers in traditional homes made them more difficult to train, especially in domestic duties. These obstacles soon forced Baird to retreat, and by 1880 the Odanah boarding school accepted only boys, "who pretty clearly have a call to the work." Those few girls who attended classes did so in the day school.[39]

This pattern held true for Odanah and its outstations as well. Boys outnumbered girls on most available monthly or quarterly school reports.[40] Although the missionaries flirted with the idea of reopening a female school, their plans never materialized. Night classes at both Odanah and Round Lake admitted only young men and boys. As one teacher explained, "The young men have been anxious that I should have an evening school as they find the need especially of Arithmetic since being brought in business relations with the whites."[41]

The Odanah mission and its satellites struggled to survive after the BFM takeover in 1872. Day school enrollments rarely exceeded twenty students, and the boarding school fared even worse. The situation had not been improved by the refusal of the Office of Indian Affairs to cover costs of the day school, because the BFM took it over on its own initiative.[42] Baird also reported in 1883 that the death rate had been extremely high: a quarter of the local Ojibwa population had died. The remaining people, especially the elderly, seemed "almost desperate and defiant at times."[43] Baird finally resigned in 1884, consumed by a sense of uselessness. "No more young men come forward to study," he mourned, and active missionary work effectively ended at the central mission.[44]

Odanah did not improve under the tenure of Francis Spees, whose rigid approach and poor management alienated Indians and whites alike. Following Spees's transfer to the Lac du Flambeau outstation, Henry Blatchford, now an elderly minister, assumed responsibility for Odanah, but his age prevented him from performing more than Sunday duties. Interestingly, Blatchford believed the actions of one of the white mission teachers had thoroughly alienated native women by 1886. Earlier that year Minnie Ells, one of Peter and Maria Dougherty's daughters, had, at the instigation of another white woman, gone about dressed as a man. "She has lost all the respect due her from the women at this place as missionary & teacher," Blatchford angrily reported; "even boys call her little man when they see her walking any where."[45] The mission's course never smoothed out, and in 1886, as part of a policy change, the Presbyterian church transferred Odanah to the Board of Home Missions, whereupon it became a domestic church serving a primarily white congregation.[46]

This same pattern of initial success followed by decline held at the BFM's Omena mission in Michigan's Lower Peninsula, where Peter Dougherty and Rev. John Fleming had settled to proselytize the area north of Grand Rapids. Primarily Ottawa territory, these lands had, according to tradition, been ceded to the Ojibwa in compensation for a murder in the late eighteenth century, although some Ottawa remained.[47] When Fleming departed following his wife's sudden death in 1839, Dougherty assumed responsibility for the newly established mission.

A graduate of Princeton Theological Seminary, Old School in his orientation and training, Dougherty was conservative and committed to the ideas of work, property, and moral order. The BFM demanded "deep piety, genuine personal holiness, and singleness of purpose" of its missionaries and an unswerving dedication to perfecting the spiritual, moral, and physical condition of the heathens; Peter Dougherty was such a man.[48] Anxious to remedy his lonely status as a bachelor as well as to gain a helpmate, Dougherty wrote to his friend Daniel Wells:

> The first and most important and indispensible thing that I need and desire and which you will be pleased to procure and forward with as little delay as possible is a good *wife*. One of devoted spirit, willing to go any where and to do any thing for the glory of the Savior in the Salvation of immortal souls. Let her be a person of cultivated mind, amiable disposition, not destitute of personal charm, not too aenal [aenan (brazen)?] or elevated, having energy of character, a good constitution and in age ranging between twenty and twenty-eight.[49]

Within the year he had married Maria Higgins, with whom he raised eight daughters and a son at the mission.

The mission originated at Grand Traverse and included day and boarding schools and a farm; during the next few years the BFM opened satellite stations at nearby Little Traverse, Bear Creek, and Middle Village. When the Ojibwa relocated to Grove Hill in 1862, Dougherty followed them. The Ojibwa called the new mission Omena ("it is so")—which, they claimed, was Dougherty's stock response to all their questions. Dougherty eventually capitulated and also referred to the mission as Omena.[50]

Despite some initial opposition from shamans and medicine men, overall Dougherty was roundly welcomed by the local males. When he had been scouting for a site, the chief of a small village at Manistee eagerly asked to have his community included in the mission's territory; Dougherty reported to Walter Lowrie, corresponding secretary of the BFM, that "the chief is an amiable man who is very desirous to have a school established in his village. He embraces every opportunity of learning, and he is adopting the customs of white men—he would do all he could to induce his people to improve."[51] Chiefs near Little Traverse were delighted that the BFM was setting up stations near them and expressed great hope that Dougherty would instruct their sons in English.[52]

Once he was established, the men were quick to come by and look over the minister's offerings. At the first services in his new station, Dougherty had quite a good audience, all male. As he reported to Daniel Wells,

> I went over and held a meeting at which there was a general attendance of the men who listened with attention and apparent interest. The second day I opened a School in the little house which the Chief had provided for me. You would have been much interested to have seen how men and children gathered round to receive instruction. They manifest great interest to learn and are untiring in application.[53]

The older boys even came at night for lessons, and the principal men of the community attended worship whenever they were in the village.

At a series of revival meetings in 1842, ten Ojibwa (gender unspecified) declared themselves saved at the first session. A second meeting netted an even greater catch: sixteen came forward to accept the gospel, including Chief Aghosa, a powerful man in the community. The following year, Aghosa was baptized and acquired the unlikely name of Addison Potts. His conversion inspired another leader, dubbed the "Old Chief" by Dougherty, to attend religious inquiry classes with his wife.[54] Although Dougherty only randomly listed converts by gender in his letters to BFM headquarters, correspondence from Andrew Porter, J. G. Turner, and Walter Guthrie at the satellite missions of Bear Creek, Middle Village, and Little Traverse indicate a preponderance of male converts, as did Isaac Baird's letters from Odanah.[55]

An episode in the late 1850s indicates the intensity with which some men adopted their new faith. For some time Dougherty had had problems with young men "crying and hollowing and making a great noise in the prayer meetings held at Mr Greensky's" (Edwin Green Sky, a Methodist, was his interpreter). When he finally asked them in 1859 to temper their unabashedly fervent worship, the young men retorted that they "would not discontinue their rowdy meeting but after mine in the church the[y] would have theirs at Green-skys." Dougherty then threatened to fire his interpreter if he supported the rebels. When Green Sky brazenly ignored Dougherty's orders, the missionary had to back down, for he had no other interpreter.[56] Green Sky and the young men soon cut their ties with the mission. Some congregants suspected the Methodist of having planned the split all along. Dougherty pragmatically decided that it was simply the "natural result of excitement they have not properly governed," but the young men's betrayal wounded him nonetheless.[57] "I deeply regret the course those young men have taken," he lamented; "I loved them and do Still for they are the most consistent and intelligent & lively Christians in our church—They have left us, seldom, some never, coming to our meetings." The schism was never mended, and the separatists later joined the Methodist camp meetings in nearby North Point.[58]

These upheavals seemed to pass women by, however. Although they rarely openly opposed the Presbyterians, in a few instances they made what might have been subtle gestures against the missionaries; for instance, they refused to wear non-Indian dresses sent to the mission for them, preferring their traditional dress.[59] (This attitude was not limited to Ojibwa women. Sue McBeth, Presbyterian missionary to the Nez Perce in Kamiah, Idaho, reported that women there often insisted on wearing "squaw" dress.)[60] When Andrew Porter, a teacher at the Grand Traverse satellite mission of Bear River, solicited contributions for the Presbyterian Choctaw mission in Oklahoma Indian Territory, only two of the twenty-two Ojibwa contributors were women.[61] Dougherty's letters suggest that at Omena, unlike at Odanah, women generally did not participate in prayer sessions. The women who converted, moreover, were often wives or daughters of leading Christians and probably pressured by their husbands' example. Others were girls from the mission schools who had accepted Christian teachings; Dougherty and Porter each admitted present or former female students into the church. Even these, however, were few in number. Female students were simply hard to come by.[62]

The missionaries puzzled over the shortage of girls in the schools, having had no difficulty recruiting boys. Starting with

Dougherty's first contacts in the late 1830s, Ojibwa men had sought to educate their sons. In fact, their openness to the missionaries arose largely from the significance they attached to American schooling, particularly the opportunity to learn English. Even Dougherty realized that Aghosa and others at Grand Traverse wanted him as much for the instruction he could provide as for his ministerial work.[63]

In 1840, Dougherty reported to Henry Schoolcraft that the older boys attended classes twice daily and gladly immersed themselves in evening and daytime instruction. By the early 1850s, his work had elicited widespread interest among the men of Little Traverse; one had even implored the missionary to educate his two sons in Dougherty's own home. In 1851, ten men decided that their children must learn English, and they petitioned Dougherty to start a school in Little Traverse. Catholic men from Middle Village and a chief from Cheboygan braved excommunication in 1853 to have Presbyterian schools started in their communities. That same year, twenty-three men from Cross Village (a defunct Jesuit mission reopened in 1825) petitioned the BFM to send a resident teacher to give their children an "English education."[64] In each case, Dougherty attributed the requests to a growing appreciation of the value of American tutelage.

Dougherty did not neglect the girls; indeed, he attempted to lure students to a female school staffed by women teachers and designed to train girls to be good Christians with proper domestic skills.[65] At first the school seemed a hit: the initial enrollment in 1848 stood at twenty-two, and several girls even brought their mothers to afternoon sewing classes. Within two years, however, attendance had dwindled to a handful. While the boys' school flourished with twenty students at least, the girls' school had at best ten. Perturbed by the paucity of female students, which he thought might be due to an overall decline in the number of local girls that winter, the minister wrote in 1850: "Since New Years there have been so few girls who attended school I thought it might be as well closed for the present."[66]

Female recruitment still lagged; when Dougherty opened a manual labor boarding school in 1853, twenty-two boys en-

rolled, "but few Girls."[67] The five girls who did attend were
far from satisfactory students. "We have had less trouble with
our boys than the girls," the missionary complained. "We have
had considerable trouble with some of our larger girls."[68] Over
the next few years, enrollments improved somewhat, but by
1860 Dougherty admitted to Lowrie that while the boys' school
was full, "there are but few girls offering to come." This predic-
ament continued, with an overall ratio of two boys for every girl
student.[69] While it is certainly possible that simple demograph-
ics regulated female enrollments, or that women needed their
daughters to work at home, Dougherty may have misinter-
preted the issues. The BFM's thwarted efforts at Middle Village
suggest that the school's lack of success in recruiting girls may
have reflected women's reluctance to accept education.

In 1853, at the request of the chief at Middle Village, the
BFM hired J. G. Turner to begin a school in the community. To
gain a competitive edge over nearby Catholics and to entice students to his day school, Turner fed them free lunches: "Thanks
be to God for his mercy: we attribute our success, under Him,
to the excellent plan of giving victuals, you know it is the
'soupers', who get the blame of turning so many in Ireland . . .
it [providing meals] tends to strengthen every tie, and where
scholars are scarce, it will bring them in."[70] The young men of
the village soon demanded night classes as well and willingly
cut wood and provided lamps for heat and light to work by.
When the Catholic bishop threatened to excommunicate any
Ojibwa who attended Presbyterian services, Turner was forced
to stop all religious instruction so that his students might stay
with their lessons; nonetheless, he felt he had gained a foot-
hold. "That first year," he recalled, "many of the young men
and some of the children attended the Sabbath."[71]

These rather satisfying circumstances deteriorated, however,
when Rev. Hugh Walter Guthrie arrived in 1856 to serve as
minister to the combined outstations. Within the year, attendance at the school and services in Middle Village had dropped
precipitously. Indeed, Turner reported with some irritation,
now "the people and children actually think that they are doing
us a favor to come to School at all."[72] Guthrie blamed the
nearby Catholic priest; Turner was at a loss. "I felt in hope that

Mr Guthrie would meet with some encouragement here," Turner wrote Lowrie in a troubled letter. "Last Sabbath there were three out from . . . 10. and 15 make up the usual number that attend. No woemen or children of this number. All men." He should, he commented with disgust and frustration, just have stayed in Ohio.[73]

Conditions at Middle Village finally grew so unpromising that the BFM decided to close the station entirely. Very few people attended Sabbath services, and school was canceled after only one day in September 1857 owing to lack of students. Guthrie morbidly wrote the situation off as hopeless: "I am losing mental strength and activity every day," he lamented, and querulously requested a transfer.[74]

When faced with the impending demise of their school, however, the Ojibwa men quickly rallied. "Our hearts are in distress. . . . We are poor ignorant Indians and did not know our duty in regard to the School," their spokesman, Gosegwad, wrote in an imploring letter to the executive committee of the BFM.[75] The men, although they acknowledged that the board had ample reason for closing the station, vowed to send the children regularly henceforth. Turner, however, was not persuaded. "I must say for these Indian Men," he conceded,

> that I believe them sincere and that they earnestly desire to have their children come to our school. *But the trouble is with the woemen. . . . We can always get the men together at almost any time to talk to them but the woemen we cant reach.* Therefore I think that the promises from the men however sincere they may be will not amount to much. (my emphasis)

And he observed once again how discouraging the recent years had been and that "the woemen and children have not attended at all on the Sabbath or but very little."[76]

Turner now began to accuse the Catholics of causing his problems. He alleged that priests had held the women under their sway ever since Frederic Baraga opened a Catholic mission on the west shore of L'Anse Bay in 1835, hoping to establish a "reduction" based on the French Jesuit plan in Canada. Baraga had purchased some five hundred acres and promised local Christian Indians that he would build houses for them if they became sedentary.[77] Guthrie had long condemned priests and nuns as a "clan of soul destroyers doing their deeds of death and damnation."[78] And Andrew Porter had worried that they would teach the Indians "all the abomination of their corrupt system . . . since the priests are untirring [*sic*] in their efforts to corrupt the minds of these poor people."[79] Like most contemporary Protestants, Turner and the others brooded that the spread of Roman Catholicism would perpetuate heathenism of a variety more malevolent than the aboriginal. "We have to fight the fearfully parallizing influence of the R. Catholics inch by inch, year in and year out," Baird's successor at Odanah would later proclaim, "in its attempt to mix idolotry with true religion."[80]

The ministers also believed, with some justification, that the priests did not share their conviction regarding the need for congregants to abandon traditional Ojibwa practices. The Catholics had a less rigidly ethnocentric approach to proselytization than the Presbyterian; rather than demanding that Indians totally reject their heritage, they sought common denominators in native religion and emphasized those.[81] Although the BFM missionaries believed that the Catholics were protecting Ojibwa beliefs and had encouraged the women's hostility to Presbyterian efforts, only after the station closed did the Protestant missionaries broaden the charge to credit the opposition with the power to convert and manipulate all the women.

It is not surprising that Guthrie and Turner quickly blamed women's resistance on the baneful influence of local Catholics: the priests, after all, provided an easy and familiar scapegoat. Moreover, the situation was undoubtedly a disconcerting one. Women would not participate in Presbyterian services or sanction the mission school. The missionaries, in their search for an explanation, must have found it far easier to castigate the opposition than to entertain the notion that the women themselves spurned their offer of salvation and civilization.[82] Turner may have interpreted the situation correctly; perhaps Catholicism, which had been established in the area for some time, did provoke women's refusal to patronize the Presbyterian mission. If so, the question remains why women opposed the Protestants while their husbands, brothers, and sons defied priestly admonitions and attended BFM services and schools. Probably, allegiance to Catholicism allowed women to maintain some native religion and practices, which Protestants demanded they abandon.

By 1861 Peter Dougherty believed that his mission, too, must close within a few years; the previous year had produced no inquiries, let alone conversions. Throughout the Civil War the school operated at a loss, and in 1866 the BFM instructed Dougherty to sell.[83] Reluctant to abandon the forty regular church members, he continued to maintain the church, but by 1870 he had to admit defeat. The Ojibwa population had dwindled owing to relocations and deaths, an oil company was prospecting nearby, and white settlers now controlled much of the area. In 1871, the BFM closed Omena and the Bear River outstation; the organization's precarious financial status did not allow it to continue supporting Indian missions without Indians. Dougherty's last letters were peppered with reports that drums and dances still sounded among the remaining Ojibwa; although the women of Omena and Odanah were not blamed for the missions' demise (unlike at Middle Village), clearly their efforts to keep traditional ways alive had been successful.[84]

Women's reluctance to support the BFM likely came from concerns about the destructive potential of mission schooling and the threat it posed to their daughters' socialization and to the cultural integrity of their communities. Although women have no voice in the Middle Village records, a monthly report filed in 1885 from the Round Lake mission by two of the Doughertys' daughters, Susie and Cornelia, specifically stated that women were indeed fearful. "We have hope that the Angels are rejoicing with us over the conversion of a woman who two or three weeks ago gave herself to Jesus and seems like a new woman. God is very good to us—May this be but the first of many souls to be saved here," they wrote.[85] They went on to say that this first conversion had led them to hope that they might finally be "gaining a little hold upon the women," who had so far rebuffed them. The incident proved to be unusual, however. Susie's postscript to the report supplied a startling commentary on the women's reticence: "I asked a young [man] one day not long ago how this truth [that they were gaining some ground with the women] appeared to him he answered [']I think of it—but—I do not know whether it is true—but as our own Christian woman Elizabeth says *they are afraid of the thing*. Do not be discouraged they will listen and accept the Light in time[']" (my emphasis).[86] This young man's interpretation suggests that women had concerns about the effects of Christianity and education and that men were aware of, but uninfluenced by, women's fears.

This was not an isolated event. Father Anthony Maria Gachet, a Swiss Capuchin who worked among the Wisconsin Menomini (Central Algonquians who shared numerous cultural traits with Ojibwa) from 1859 to 1862, also observed that women appeared to hate Christianity and its representatives. He described a couple who had fought bitterly over the issue of conversion. "The husband had decided for a long time before to 'take the prayer' but the hatred that his wife bore to the Christians prevented him from realizing his vows," the priest recorded in his journal.[87] The woman finally decided to convert only when it became clear that, as a Christian, her husband could not remain married to a pagan.

Gachet also related the fury of a woman whose newly converted son-in-law had abandoned her daughter for a Christian wife (although his first wife would have converted to keep him). As the man was leaving with his new spouse, Gachet observed that

> the mother of the abandoned wife, pagan herself, met them. She is a virago who handles an oar and hunting piece as easily as our warriors. With eye on fire she addressed to the culpable Christian these words: "Infamous girl, I am very glad to meet you. . . . Ah, fortunate for you that I fear the Mékata-Koneia (black robe, missionary), otherwise I would tear you to pieces. Thank him that I fear him, but take care if I meet you again. This fear may not find itself in my heart. Then nothing will restrain me."[88]

It seems that while men viewed education and conversion as an advantage, women saw Christianity, schools, and clergy as a threat, and the mission schoolhouse became a silent battleground. Even a cursory examination of the nineteenth-century mission school suggests its impact on children suddenly removed from native life-styles and the menace it presented to women who abruptly lost control of their daughters' educations. Their distrust of missions and schools was not unfounded. Protestant missionaries, and Presbyterians in particular, wanted "to bring the depraved and degraded people around them under the influence of the Christian religion."[89] By removing children from their parents' influence, missionaries could create a new, assimilated generation for whom Ojibwa culture no longer existed. Isaac Baird, for example, banned Ojibwa language in the classroom; to him it represented ignorance and superstition. He believed that if the school rigorously demanded English, Ojibwa would be obsolete within twenty years. "The children [must be] gotten clean out of all their own old wild ways & immured to the customs of civilized life," he concluded. "This can only be *effectually* accomplished by taking them away from the demoralizing & enervating atmosphere of camp life & Res. surroundings & concomitants."[90]

The Presbyterians saw the obliteration of traditional culture not as a destructive process, but as a crucial step in creating Westernized individuals who conformed to the social expectations and gender roles of American culture. Although convinced of the degradation of "heathen" culture and the need to replace it with gospel truths, many evangelists did not think Indians were inferior as persons. As Andrew Porter, arriving in Grand Traverse in 1847 en route to Little Traverse, informed his uncle, Walter Lowrie,

> This people are very interesting, their simplicity of manners, their accommodating disposition, and their general good nature makes them, not only objects of pity, as I was ready to suppose, but also of esteem. Many of them are men of good sense, and great discerners of character: and those who act right toward them, may hope to gain their friendship and love.[91]

Because the missionaries were sure that the native population was disappearing, they assumed responsibility for averting this impending disaster and for rescuing Indians from extinction. Isaac Baird wrote from Odanah that "the Indians are fast fading away. What is done for them must be done quickly. It seems to me," he optimistically estimated, "if the Presb. Church of this land, would only stir herself just a little, all the Agencies open to her evangelizing effort might be Christianized before 1,900 A.D." He concluded by imploring that the church send its "munificent gifts" for "these perishing heathens at our doors."[92] Baird wanted to prepare Ojibwa for school, work, and church in white America. Insisting that "isolation for the Indian will hereafter be impracticable," the missionary maintained that "he must be absorbed must meet and become part and parcel of American civilization. The problem of his admixture with the white race presses for speedy solution."[93]

Ministers and lay teachers instructed children in a broad range of subjects geared toward a mainstream American lifestyle: grammar, history, natural sciences, and other standard courses for white children were combined with instruction in farming for boys and in domestic skills such as sewing, knitting, and housekeeping for girls. The mission schools' goal for girls was to direct them away from the world of the native woman, away from the autonomy and prestige of females in traditional life, and toward the responsibilities of Christian womanhood with its emphasis on female piety, domesticity, submissiveness, and the patriarchal nuclear family. This aim required that girls be removed from the influence of their mothers as much as possible, placed under the direction of white women, and introduced to Western gender roles, values, and work.

As far as the missionaries were concerned, native women were "ignorant of work and careless and dirty in their habits," and their influence on daughters was strictly negative.[94] Although women's responsibilities were many and varied, seasonal nomadism and its concomitant light household inventory left Ojibwa women without the daily grind of domestic upkeep that was so much a part of middle-class American life. "An Indian female has but little of the work to do about house, which we missionaries think ought to be done, if we would retain the rudiments of civilized life," reported one minister. "She has no house to clean—few clothes to make, none to mend and none to wash."[95] Missionaries, convinced that the more "home comforts" native women had, the more industrious and civilized they would become, were determined to change this situation for the rising generation by familiarizing them with permanent housing, Western dress, and a desire for manufactured material goods.[96] What the ministers did not take into account, however, was that once a child had left school and returned to the village or reservation, most students had little opportunity to apply the domestic and academic instruction to which they had been exposed; girls, in particular, unless they lived in the rare frame house, could exercise their newfound housekeeping skills only by becoming domestic servants for whites in nearby communities or at the missions themselves.

Formal religious instruction in Christianity was, of course, integral to the curriculum, which constantly promoted Protestant beliefs and values. This separation of religious doctrine from the general activities of daily life contrasted greatly with the native belief system, which saw no division between the material and spiritual worlds. Values, rituals, and techniques for communicating with supernaturals were woven into the fabric of daily life rather than isolated and organized into dogmatic primers.

Missionaries measured the success of religious instruction by the number of converts among pupils. This indoctrination apparently often succeeded at least in securing the students' submission to its dictates, as compositions by Indian children published in the Presbyterian journal *Foreign Missionary* suggest. A young girl's reaction to a traditional burial ritual bore witness to the impact of her education: "On one occasion when a woman had died," she wrote, "two of these mourning women came and commenced wailing so mournfully that the children were very much annoyed, and as they had been at the mission they were ashamed of this heathen practice."[97] Removed from intimate daily contact with their mothers and placed in schools for long days or even months, this child and her classmates felt compelled to deny the rituals and beliefs that their mothers' generation observed and cherished.[98]

The expectation that converts would renounce native practices compounded the threat of mission schools. "As soon as any individual bows to the authority of Gods Word and accepts Jesus Christ as a personal Savior, that person at once abandons all the old heathen ways," Baird explained to a government Indian agent, "and at once enters upon the duties and activities of

civilized life, in so far as they are accessible."[99] Although Baird
undoubtedly exaggerated the degree to which converts repudiated tradition, his comment made it clear that Ojibwa Christians were to embrace civilization along with the Savior. As
Francis Spees, Baird's successor at Odanah, observed, Ojibwa
themselves believed that those who attended prayer meetings
had discarded native religion.[100]

Another challenge faced by girls and their mothers was the
classroom itself. Native education was not confined to a schoolhouse but took place constantly, in lectures and councils,
through listening, in working with elders or imitating their activities in play. Little girls helped their mothers carry water or
clean dishes; they mimicked women skilled in tanning, beadwork, gathering and preparing medicinal plants, and other
tasks. Mother and child worked closely and companionably together as the daughter learned the skills of female life. Grandmothers played an important role in girls' education as well,
particularly in advising them and in telling stories that illus-
trated traditional values and history. Often during the winter a
woman sent a child to her grandmother with a present of tobacco in exchange for instruction in the myths that explained
to the girl her place in the Ojibwa world.[101]

The interest that many Ojibwa men expressed in education
indicates that they agreed with Baird's assessment that American civilization had to be accepted, at least in part. While it is
unlikely that most men either desired or anticipated complete
absorption into white society, they apparently concluded that
schooling would enable them to deal more successfully with the
growing white population. Men, rather than women, inter-
acted most closely with whites through transactions in lumber,
mining, or land and negotiations with government Indian
agencies. It was clearly to their advantage, therefore, to cultivate a relationship with Presbyterian missionaries, who could
give them access to the powerful tool of literacy. By 1860, for
example, Andrew Porter reported from Bear River that virtually all the men could read. His classes always had more males
than females, often more than twice the number.[102] Less than
half the women in the community could read, and those only
poorly; they evidently did not share the men's desire to acquire

skills in English. As a result, males and females increasingly diverged in the value they placed on native culture, as the missionaries' reports of men's wish to marry girls from the schools suggests.[103]

At heart, however, the last experiments had failed. Women's reluctance to accept mission education or Christian beliefs encouraged continued adherence to native ritual practices, especially among the female population. Indeed, early-twentieth-century ethnographies suggest that as male and female interests and needs further diverged—largely as a result of differences in the nature and degree of Indians' interaction with the dominant society—both sexes increasingly viewed women as the conservators of traditional ways.

6

SEPARATE WORLDS

By the late nineteenth century many missionary organizations, plagued by funding problems similar to those of the Wesleyan Methodists and Presbyterians, curtailed their pursuit of Native American converts. Systematic efforts to proselytize Ojibwa subsided for several decades, and in the Upper Great Lakes, native communities again slipped into a period of limited association with white society.[1] The respite proved brief, however, for at this juncture a new breed of missionaries arrived—not evangelicals, but anthropologists. Intent on recording rather than eliminating native culture and armed with psychological theories and instruments, researchers such as Ruth Landes and A. Irving Hallowell collected individual histories and examined the lives of Ojibwa in minute detail. Their analyses became classic portraits of communities that, torn by gender hostility, found themselves unable to unite against the depredations of colonization.[2] These ethnologies, however, reflected the assumptions and practices of early-twentieth-century anthropology; they dealt only with the ethnographic present, creating ahistorical portraits of Ojibwa society. Landes, for example, discussed Ojibwa men going out in war parties, yet she did her fieldwork in the 1930s, long after active intertribal warfare had ceased.[3]

The growth of anthropology as an academic field in the late nineteenth century paralleled the expansion of evolutionary theory from the natural into the social sciences. Lewis Henry Morgan and others expected to trace the development of human society by comparing living tribal cultures to "modern" civilization.[4] Data salvage was top priority and, they believed, would unveil the social evolution of human traits and cultural structures. In the 1890s, however, Franz Boas and his adherents, pioneers in the field of cultural anthropology, rejected this conjectural approach and the scientific racism in which it was based in favor of cultural determinism. A new breed, these social scientists sought out "primitive" peoples throughout the world, their mission being to preserve native beliefs, customs, and material culture. Yet they too believed that the spread of Western civilization heralded the end of Indian culture, that acculturation and assimilation would eliminate Native Americans as tribal peoples. These anthropologists' goal, therefore, was to map the inner workings of "primitive" cultures before the tribes disappeared, and in their attempts to acquire inside knowledge of religion, rituals, and social relations their data-collecting methods frequently verged on ruthless.[5] In the process, they sometimes indiscriminately mixed elements of contemporary and traditional life, oblivious to the impact of colonization and intercultural contact.

Both Hallowell and Landes assumed that Ojibwa culture as they observed it was essentially aboriginal. Hallowell acknowledged that traders and missionaries had tried to initiate acculturation, but he implied that the Ojibwa had only recently abandoned ritual practices or strayed from older cultural norms.[6] Landes did not give even Hallowell's cursory nod to change. Although she carried out her research in western Ontario and northwestern Minnesota in the 1930s, she maintained that the internal aspect of Ojibwa life remained basically unchanged: "They lived still much as their forebears had a century earlier, except that their hazardous subsistence had worsened from encroachments of white settlers. Hunters and food-gatherers, ever threatened by starvation and disease, they were profoundly religious."[7]

Hallowell and Landes both were struck by an overwhelming sense of dichotomy in Ojibwa culture. It was a polarized world awash in oppositions and contradictions—bush and camp, plenty and starvation, good and evil supernaturals. Infiltrating all these categories was a pervasive division between male and female. Holding the upper hand in ritual activities and social prestige, it seemed, were men; it was they whose lives required and received "supernatural validation."[8] Men, Hallowell insisted, "were the approved mediators between the supernatural world and mankind."[9]

Hallowell essentially brushed women off into a spiritual limbo. Men, he said, were hunters whose precarious calling demanded an intense relationship with supernatural beings, upon which their self-esteem depended. They were empowered yet exposed, open to failure. If a community's survival rested entirely on the outcome of men's hunting, as Hallowell and Landes incorrectly assumed (later studies showed that small game snared by women and children was a substantial part of the diet), the focal point of ritual life must be male rapport with game animals.[10] Women could thus be little more than observers of the ritual world of men. "A woman's life being primarily domestic," Hallowell suggested, "[it] does not necessitate all the safeguards about her ego that men develop"; as a result, "women do not feel so vulnerable in their self-respect."[11] Women could seek supernatural aid, but no cultural imperatives demanded that they do so or rewarded them for successfully cultivating spiritual relationships. Women's psychological security, he decided, came from human rather than superhuman contacts.

Landes and Hallowell both believed that Ojibwa society reserved its honors for men. "Whenever men fulfill their duties creditably, they are lauded," observed Landes. "Even the mythology occupies itself with the pursuits and rewards of men. The important visions, which men have been driven all their youth to pursue, bestow power for the masculine occupations."[12] Tradition controlled men's lives, she insisted, but "the female half is left to spontaneous and confused behavior."[13] Women's daily and life cycle rituals had only minimal importance, since men did not participate in them. Even women's participation in the Midewiwin, or Medicine Lodge, Landes maintained, was in the context of lesser roles, to which men had relegated them. To Landes, Ojibwa culture was a ranked system of social and spiritual roles, one that "laid down a glamorous course for men" but considered women to be "second-rate, or perhaps reserve material."[14] She believed this hierarchy of social worth was a continuation of both traditional patterns of interaction between men and women and an ancient belief system.

What Landes was witnessing, however, was in fact the outcome of a historical process that retained the older framework
for social and spiritual relations while altering much of the
intrinsic meaning of those relations. It was, to use Eric Hobsbawm's phrase, an invented tradition, which spoke to the
changes that had taken place in Ojibwa culture in the wake of
increasingly complex contact with white America.[15] Hobsbawm
has suggested that in times of rapid social change factions mine
older symbolism or ritual to "invent" fictitious traditions, which
they then use to establish values and behavioral norms that le-
gitimize their position in the new social order. Among the
Ojibwa, the newly created "tradition" of gender hostility and
symbolic polarity was a symptom of changes that had taken
place in the social relationships of women and men. Building
on the older, parallel complementarity between male and female, it validated the status changes in Ojibwa communities
that arose from what Hobsbawm would call the "social engi-
neering" of missionaries' efforts to eliminate the traditional system and from the forces of ecoenvironmental change.

Many traditional patterns had continued: boys still were tu-
tored by their fathers in the skills of the hunt, and girls were instructed by mothers and grandmothers in the responsibilities
of the camp. Female interests and expectations continued to be
unique from those of males. The difference was that these distinctions, the separate ways and values, no longer had a com-
parable significance that was accepted throughout the community. Now the discrete yet connected roles of men and women
had been sundered, polarized—assigned differing merit by
each gender. Landes described, with a poignancy she herself
may not have realized, the gulf between male and female:

> Mothers and daughters discuss the merits of their work just as men
> do the merits of theirs, and when the village quarter of the year
> comes about, the various families visit, and wider groups of women
> discuss their own interests. But these discussions and boasts are not
> formal, as the men's are; they belong to the level of gossip.
>   . . . In the absence of the men, the women form a closed world
> where each woman is distinctive, where women's work is valued
> explicitly, and where women's values are pursued. It is complete-
> ly dissociated from the world of men where women's work is

conventionally ignored and where no individual woman is distinc-
tive. In the relaxed smoking hours after the hunt and at the feasts,
men talk about the "important" things within their experience. . . .
In their continuous busy hours, while the men are gone from the
lodge, women talk about *their* important experiences.[16]

In some ways, women and men were at a standoff. Social relations were uneasy, even hostile. Men viewed women with distrust; they were particularly fearful of female "power" during
menstruation, which now had malevolent rather than pro-
found connotations. (Neighboring Menomini men expressed
similar fear of women, claiming they could be "killers of men's
power.")[17] Women in turn taught their daughters to distrust
men and regarded displays of male spiritual weakness or inad-
equacy with a pity verging on contempt.[18] Antagonism and
fragile marriages characterized sexual relationships. Landes
and Hallowell both commented on the pervasive aura of conflict, as well as noting the comparison between courtship and
hunting. Although women decided when sexual relations would
take place, Landes remarked, "the phrase for flirting is 'hunting women,' which uses the same verb as 'hunting meat.' " She
and Hallowell both interpreted this linguistic fact as a sign of
long-standing cultural male dominance.[19]

But these conclusions clearly contradict what the historical
record tells us about gender relations in communities just coming into contact with Euro-American culture. There appears,
rather, to be an invented tradition of male supremacy, one that
speaks to an increasing sense of separation and mistrust between men and women. This polarity reflected changing social,
economic, and cosmological relationships. Male and female
now inhabited segregated worlds, shared few goals; life was
asymmetrical, antagonistic. Men and women saw themselves as
different beings with separate, even conflicting roles. What had
at one time been culturally sanctioned and virtually positive
gender complementarity had been exaggerated as male and female experiences diverged into mutually exclusive, separate
spheres—spheres remarkably similar to those promoted by
missionaries. With the increase in interaction with white society
during the nineteenth century, the difference in male and fe-

male experiences of colonization, evident from the Jesuit through the Presbyterian Ojibwa missions, was evolving into the dichotomized society that the anthropologists described.

Hallowell, in fact, observed that the men he studied had lost confidence in native beliefs under the impact of white influence and that their world, always vulnerable, had grown more unstable. As males gradually moved from the old ways toward an acceptance of Christianity and education, women increasingly identified themselves, and were so identified by men, with traditional culture. In some ways this change protected women's status and interests, for the very separateness of the female world helped preserve it from the disintegration that often devastated the lives of men. Indeed, this separation became so pervasive that it effectively hid women's lives from observers. As a result, ethnologists, whose male-oriented training certainly contributed to the situation, remained unaware of the scope, significance, or continuity of the ritual world of female culture.[20] Landes and Hallowell saw without seeing that women had a spiritual and social identity independent of men. Women's world—their rituals, concerns, and traditions—remained viable, though not unchanged; still valued by women, if not by men.

Ethnographies by Diamond Jenness, Frank Speck, and Frances Densmore, contemporaries of Hallowell and Landes, further suggest that gender dichotomy is a historical phenomenon of colonization. The Parry Island Ojibwa and Montagnais-Naskapi studied by Speck and Jenness, and the Minnesota, Wisconsin, and Manitou Rapids (Ontario) Ojibwa observed by Densmore (and later by Sister M. Inez Hilger), maintained an isolation from white culture that enabled them to retain more traditional lifeways than the Minnesota, Western Ontario, and Berens River Ojibwa studied by Landes and Hallowell.[21] The Parry Island and Montagnais-Naskapi communities still stressed gender distinctions rather than dichotomy, reciprocity rather than antagonism. The contributions of male and female were valued, and the boundaries between them had remained flexible: each had characteristics unique to their sex but was free to engage in activities designated to the other. In the 1930s, for example, Montagnais-Naskapi women freely hunted as desire or occasion demanded. "Women are neither physically nor spiritually disqualified from the pursuit of game, as frequent testimony proves," Speck explained. Many women hunted, some throughout their lives, and, like one old woman who hung the skulls of bear and beaver she had killed outside her wigwam, dreamed of game and propitiated the supernaturals.[22] Twenty years later, Eleanor Leacock found among the Montagnais-Naskapi that this same flexibility persisted and the existence of gender-defined tasks did not prevent one sex from doing the work of the other if needed.[23] In contrast, the Ojibwa men whom Landes observed, she said, never deviated from rigidly delineated "male" functions. Any women who performed male activities were believed to do so only because females lacked strong cultural guidelines for individual life.

Parry Islanders and Montagnais-Naskapi also appeared to be free of the inelastic ritual boundaries that governed men and women in the communities studied by Landes and Hallowell. Once married, Parry Island women joined with men in dances and feasts, and Montagnais women evoked the hunt as they drummed and sang. Jenness and Hilger, moreover, observed that the quest for supernatural power marked both male and female, and girls fasted and prayed for visions with their mothers' guidance.[24] Women blessed with visions during their menstrual seclusion had "a twofold power, the mysterious power inherent in all women and the special supernatural power derived from their visions."[25] Like that of shamans, women's power could be harmful or positive: a menstruating woman's touch turned soup to water, but then so did a baby's. Montagnais-Naskapi and Parry Island Ojibwa men guarded against a menstruating woman's power, but with respect for its strength rather than out of a fear of malevolency, which is what motivated Hallowell's and Landes's informants.[26]

Parry Island Ojibwa juxtaposed female power with other spiritual forces: it was part of a whole rather than a segregated source of fear and alienation. A sense of balance and reciprocity, rather than of asymmetry and opposition, characterized the informants' views. More recent anthropological studies seem to confirm this pattern. Leacock found relations between male and female among Montagnais-Naskapi in the 1950s to have maintained much of the flexibility that prevailed (to the Jesuits' dismay) in the early contact period. The Mistassini Cree observed by Adrian Tanner in the 1970s had two distinct religious traditions, Christian and Cree. Each operated in a separate context: Christianity in the settlements during the summer, and customary rituals in the bush during the hunting part of the year. In addition, clear distinctions were made based on gender: game animals, spatial arrangements, and the use of important objects were divided between the sexes, reflecting the roles of each in the productive activities of the bush and the camp. Nevertheless, there was no strict delineation of ritual barriers. Women practiced divination, dreamed of the hunt, and gained supernatural animal friends. Although male and female were distinct, the exchange of game animals following the hunt still provided a symbolic mediation between them.[27]

Among the Ojibwa observed by Ruth Landes, male and female clearly viewed each other as exclusive factions. Decades of missionary and trade influence and economic disadvantage had encouraged men to adapt much of the Western system; yet because that system offered no similar enticements to women, these communities became gradually divided by gender. As we have seen, the combined pressures of missionary activity, the fur trade, and environmental change exacerbated differences in male and female interests, with men finding it advantageous to participate in the fur trade, obtain at least a partial Western education, or convert. The new scheme held no such promise for women; indeed, their position in the larger society grew increasingly marginal. With complementarity sundered, men and women had diverged beyond the parameters of precontact culture.[28]

When communities such as those near the Jesuit reductions, Omena, or Odanah experienced social and economic changes that transformed gender roles, women's reliance on traditional ways became more crucial, both to their own well-being and to the survival of their communities. Their reluctance to accept many of the values and practices introduced by missionaries and their struggle to continue with customary ways (even if somewhat modified) can be seen as efforts to offset the disruptive influence of alien ideas, social structure, and technology and to maintain cultural integrity. One of the many responses of Native American communities to colonization (of which missionary work was a part), these actions also included the fierce opposition of shamans encountered by the Jesuits and the Wesleyan Methodist missionary Peter Jacobs, as well as revitalization movements such as that led by the Cree prophet Abishabis. These cultural modifications designed to preserve the status quo—or to prevent more drastic change—fit into a larger pattern of actions taken by colonized peoples. Thomas E. Harding has suggested that these "nonprogressive" adaptive shifts are defensive measures taken by all or parts of a group to avoid reorganization by outside forces and to ensure its continuity. In such situations, rather than inventing traditions to justify new roles or social orders, people place greater emphasis on older beliefs and practices anchored in the mythic past to defend the status of the group or faction as cultures clash.[29]

The introduction of Western religions, economies, and social patterns into the third world has often provided men with knowledge and skills that create both a real and symbolic male power over and above that found in the indigenous culture. Despite the increase in male authority, however, as Felicia Ifeoma Ekejiuba has observed, women remain active participants in society and often use symbolic female power to combat loss of status.[30] While scholars such as James Axtell and Christopher Vecsey have recognized the role of factionalism in Algonquian-speaking peoples' responses to colonization and to missionaries, gender has not figured prominently in their analyses.[31] Yet the historic actions of the Ojibwa and Cree communities considered in this study in many respects typify the conservative strategies Ekejiuba describes among contemporary peoples. Native women held on to traditional ritual practices, patterns of childrearing, and, to the extent possible, economic responsibilities, thereby increasing the emphasis on female values and separateness.

Women not only continued to relate creation and trickster stories, but, as the silent boycotts at Middle Village, Omena, and Odanah schools attest, they often declared themselves unwilling to support the introduction of Christianity and Western education as well. Male opposition to imposed change, in contrast, often subsided when shamans and headmen, such as those confronted by Peter Jacobs at Rainy Lake, realized that the new order offered them an opportunity to preserve their status and prestige; following their lead, many men then relinquished traditional ways as well. Women, however, were only marginal participants in that new order; an ideological defense was the only effective buffer open to them. They thus struggled to maintain "traditional" social boundaries by means of passive resistance and selective adaptations, in what Eleanor Leacock has argued is a phase of withdrawal after the initial stages of culture contact.[32]

Some scholars have suggested that Native American women, rather than resisting colonization, acted as liaisons between native and white culture. Sylvia Van Kirk, for example, found that some women in Canada deliberately sought relationships with white fur traders, for such marriages provided them with access to European technology, which they eagerly welcomed and which improved their status. As Van Kirk acknowledges, though, the number of women who aligned themselves with the trading companies through marriage was quite low. Moreover, it is reasonable that some adventuresome women would be drawn to the novelty of European-style life. Van Kirk's study and Jennifer S. H. Brown's research on women in Hudson's Bay Company families both indicate, in fact, that only a few women within one or two generations married into the trade, and their daughters made up the majority of traders' wives.[33] The other side of this point, of course, is the question of why so many women were not interested in pursuing a Euro-American life-style, an issue that Van Kirk does not satisfactorily address.

Although Van Kirk recognizes that "bourgeois European notions of how women should be treated . . . [and] of women as the fragile, weaker sex" aroused the fur traders' sympathy and even pity for native women, she does not extend the analysis to suggest that such views also colored the traders' interpretation of native women's roles.[34] Her assessment, for example, that "women in northern and woodland tribes were used as beasts of burden" and that "the division of labour in Indian society subjected the women to an endless round of domestic tasks, rendered all the more onerous by the primitive conditions of the migratory life they led," so that women's only hope of improving their lot in life was a fur trade marriage, seems a reflection of the traders' perspectives.[35] Van Kirk's assumption that women's roles were defined in terms of their relationships with men may also stem from her sources' worldview, in which women's identities were subsumed by those of males.

The question of why so few native women turned to Europeans might be addressed, as Robin Fisher suggests, by looking more closely at the cultures from which women marrying into the trade came.[36] It may be that most of these women were from groups in which women's status had entered a precipitous decline as a result of the demands of the fur trade. As Richard Perry has demonstrated for the western subarctic, women's work load rose dramatically as, in response to male expectations, they increased their processing of furs and added bundles of furs to the domestic pack loads they routinely carried.[37] The situation was, in essence, a vastly accelerated version of the process that women had experienced in seventeenth-century New France—that of becoming auxiliaries to the trade.

But older beliefs and practices remained integrated in women's daily lives; Father André's bitter remarks from Green Bay about women's support of vision quests attest to this fact, as do William Boutwell's observations regarding women's birthing and death rituals. This commitment to traditional ways was not a phenomenon specific to the Upper Great Lakes and eastern subarctic: Presbyterian missionaries to the Nez Perce of Idaho and Franciscan priests and anthropologists working among Arizona Navajo communities also commented on women's loyalty to their beliefs. Navajo women, like Ojibwa, resisted placing their children in schools and strongly objected when their husbands adopted white behavior.[38] Women also deliberately used their roles in the home to perpetuate tradition. Domesticity, in the sense of identification with hearth and children, was not an indication of insignificance, as Hallowell and Landes assumed, but a key to continuity.

Hallowell believed that women's domesticity and, as he saw it, distance from significant ritual activity protected them from the vagaries of cultural upheaval. He was, in a sense, correct, but his reasoning was off. Women were not oblivious to or unscathed by colonization; rather, the "domestic" nature of their lives was part of a carefully nurtured female identity that provided a defense against the attacks of the outside world. As mothers and keepers of the home, women were the conservators of tradition, the links between those gone before and those to follow. Daily life reflected the continuity that women treasured, and provided, for their communities. Within the closed female world depicted by Ruth Landes, women shielded traditional culture from the destructive impact of colonization even as they protected themselves. Landes herself described mothers and grandmothers as they supervised young girls, teaching them techniques for preparing food and clothing, explaining the beliefs that underlay each step, and guiding them on the paths of life.

> The days are very busy and pleasant, enlivened by stories told largely by the grandmother and mother about the work at hand: how Nenebush masqueraded as a woman and floundered about trying to do woman's work, in handicrafts and procreation. . . . how C dreamed of a new style for tailoring moccasins; how the legendary Evil Woman went out to catch a porcupine so that she might embroider her hide dress with its quills, but her foolishness was so great that she took Nenebush for a porcupine, and let him rape her while she cried, "How nice!" and finally she stood stripped while Nenebush danced in front of her and made off with her dress.[39]

Such instruction, which went hand in hand with the teaching of skilled work, not only reinforced the differences between women and men; it also reaffirmed the spiritual significance of female daily activities.

Women often geared their lives to sustaining the old ways. Jeanne Guillemin's study of Canadian Micmac (people sharing a number of culture traits with Ojibwa and Cree) who migrated between the Maritimes and Boston shows this to be particularly true of those who remained on reservations—the women responsible for the "home base." They raised their daughters to have bonds of solidarity with sisters, and females of different generations cooperated in running households and raising children. Males, however, viewed brothers in a competitive light that carried over into relationships with other adult males. Moreover, a great deal of social and sexual tension existed between men and women, who viewed themselves "as two groups rather than two individuals of the opposite sex."[40]

Women regarded the reservation home as the source of Micmac identity, the only appropriate place to rear children with traditional values. "Respectable" women did this indirectly, ostensibly clarifying the values of the dominant white society— church, education, legal marriage—and admonishing children to "act right" and follow those rules, but at the same time constantly comparing the ways of Indian and white and warning their offspring that acceptance by white society meant the loss of their Micmac identities. Indeed, as Guillemin discovered,

> a woman is good when she is respectable, not because she meets a White model of behavior, but because she brings information into the Indian culture which adds to the defenses of her children against the total society which keeps them at its periphery. It is only in her public performance that she appears to have capitulated; among her own, she has only to phrase the legal value system and let the perception of its variance with the Indian reality fall to the children, a variance which very few children fail to perceive.[41]

Even in communities where, outwardly, both sexes adopted many aspects of white culture, women's lives continued to be governed by traditional values. In her work among Menomini groups, Louise Spindler found that women who had assumed white life-styles still retained "basic, covert Menomini values" and many more aspects of Indian culture than did men. Even "assimilated" women valued native-oriented women, those still openly traditional, as living ties to their Menomini heritage.[42] Interestingly, Louise and George Spindler also concluded that women's determination to instill traditional values in their children was detrimental to men: because of the continuity and flexibility of their own roles, women did not understand or sympathize with male adjustment problems; as a result, men were suspended between the white and Indian worlds because the cultural patterns that Menomini mothers taught sons conflicted with males' need to participate in the dominant society.[43]

Similarly, Hallowell believed that Ojibwa males' identities had, shortly before the time of his study, begun to be undercut by the decline of the hunting economy and the incursions of missionaries and other whites. As trapping and hunting became increasingly less reliable as means of support, men lost many of their traditional functions. Simultaneously, women's traditional, and still viable, gathering and agricultural activities gave them an advantage over men for entering the cash economy. Among Canadian Ojibwa and Cree, the institution of family allowance payments to women had a similar effect; because the hunting practices and their accompanying rituals that men had been taught as children were no longer functional, men found themselves in a cultural limbo.[44]

Women also continued to exercise their guardianship of tradition by monitoring behavior and relationships within the community. The controlling influence of women's "gossip" struck anthropologist Regina Flannery during fieldwork among the James Bay Cree in 1933. Women frequently gathered to talk "about people, about their good as well as their bad points," excluding men from their conversations on the grounds that these were not male concerns. Despite the frivolous tag she attached to women's conversations, Flannery recognized that "gossip is an active force in their lives. It makes for conservatism, for keeping to the old ways of doing things."[45] Fear of being ostracized through gossip compelled women to wear native dress and to be conservative about sexual behavior and childrearing practices. In this way gossip both safeguarded tradition and served as a vehicle for honoring and observing values at odds with those of the larger society.

Gender issues alone, of course, did not shape the colonization experience; political, economic, and environmental factors also set the parameters for action. When economics or environment did not mandate acquiescence to colonizers' demands, communities could unite in opposition—as they did against William Boutwell and Edmund Ely. However, in the intensely polarized communities described by Landes and Hallowell it becomes evident that the gender-based divergence of interests was not aboriginal. On the contrary, the social and ideological dichotomy between male and female grew out of each sex's strategies for dealing with cultural upheaval. Women's adherence to "tradition" and men's involvement in white culture were artifacts of colonization created by the circumstances of contact. When the situation was such that women and men faced uneven futures under the new regime, when women's autonomy was directly threatened—as on the Jesuits' reductions—or quietly subverted by mission schools such as Omena or Middle Village, native women rejected Christian influences and colonial policy and pursued "traditional" lifeways. They did so to offset changes that deprived them of social, economic, and ritual parity, changes that more isolated women might temporarily circumvent but not completely elude. Women and men thus found themselves at odds, entrenched in separate confrontations with a New World hostile to the hopes and visions of both.

Notes

INTRODUCTION

1. Paula Gunn Allen, *The Sacred Hoop: Recovering the Feminine in American Indian Traditions* (Boston: Beacon Press, 1986).
2. Cecile Dauphin et al., "Women's Culture and Women's Power: An Attempt at Historiography," *Journal of Women's History* 1 (1989): 63–88, suggest that historical events in which women participated need to be reevaluated in terms of the uniqueness of an event. Although they refer specifically to political events in the Western tradition, this idea can apply as well to women's acts of resistance or accommodation to missionaries within the larger colonization process.
3. Allen, *Sacred Hoop*, 224.

CHAPTER 1

1. Reuben Gold Thwaites, ed., *The Jesuit Relations and Allied Documents: Travels and Explorations of the Jesuit Missionaries in New France, 1610–1791*, 73 vols. (Cleveland: Burrows, 1896–1901; reprinted New York: Pageant, 1959), 18:105–7 (hereafter cited as *Jesuit Relations*). New France comprised the area above the St. Lawrence from Labrador to Winnipeg.
2. Ibid., 95–107.
3. Karen Anderson, "Commodity Exchange and Subordination: Montagnais-Naskapi and Huron Women, 1600–1650," *Signs: Journal of Women in Culture and Society* 11, no. 1 (1985): 49–62.
4. *Jesuit Relations*, intro., 1:1–44.
5. Linguists have divided the Algonquian language family into two branches. The northern, Cree, branch includes the Cree, Montagnais, and Naskapi dialects; the southern, Ojibwa, branch includes the Chippewa, Saulteaux, Ottawa, and Algonquin dialects. Each branch is considered to be a single language with dialectical varieties. Cree is spoken throughout the Quebec-Labrador peninsula, the Hudson Bay coast of Ontario, central Manitoba, Saskatchewan, and Alberta. Ojibwa dialects are spoken immediately to the south, from southwest Quebec, through the upper Great Lakes, and into southern Manitoba and Saskatchewan. See Richard A. Rhodes and Evelyn M. Todd,

"Subarctic Algonquian Languages," in *Handbook of North American Indians*, vol. 6: *Subarctic*, ed. June Helm (Washington, D.C.: Smithsonian Institution, 1981), 52–66.

6. For a discussion of the potential of regional history as an alternative to studies of single "tribes," see Reginald Horsman, "Well-trodden Paths and Fresh Byways: Recent Writing on Native American History," *Reviews in American History* 10, no. 4 (1982): 234–44. See also Bruce G. Trigger, "American Archaeology as Native History: A Review Essay," *William and Mary Quarterly* 40 (1983): 413–52; Robert F. Berkhofer, Jr., "The Political Context of a New Indian History," *Pacific Historical Review* 40 (1971): 357–82.

7. For discussions of the usefulness and techniques of an ethnohistorical approach combining historical and ethnological data, see Eleanor Leacock, "Montagnais Women and the Jesuit Program for Colonization," in *Women and Colonization: Anthropological Perspectives*, ed. Mona Etienne and Eleanor Leacock (New York: Praeger, 1980), 25–42; Calvin Martin, *Keepers of the Game: Indian-Animal Relationships and the Fur Trade* (Berkeley and Los Angeles: University of California Press, 1978), 7, 71; A. Irving Hallowell, *Culture and Experience* (Philadelphia: University of Pennsylvania Press, 1955), 127; James Axtell, "Ethnohistory: A Historian's Viewpoint," in *The European and the Indian: Essays in the Ethnohistory of Colonial North America* (New York: Oxford University Press, 1981).

8. *Jesuit Relations* 5:133.

9. Ibid., 16:163. See Eleanor Leacock, "Women's Status in Egalitarian Society: Implications for Social Evolution," *Current Anthropology* 19, no. 2 (1978): 247–75, for a discussion of the problem of defining egalitarian social structure in relation to a sexual division of labor, decision making, and relationships to resources. See Anderson, "Commodity Exchange and Subordination," for a critique of Leacock.

10. For more on men's role as hunter, see Hallowell, *Culture and Experience*, 361; Ruth Landes, *Ojibwa Religion and the Midewiwin* (Madison: University of Wisconsin Press, 1968), 7, 25, 35; Ruth Landes, *The Ojibwa Woman* (New York: Norton Library, 1971), viii; Adrian Tanner, *Bringing Home Animals: Religious Ideology and Mode of Production of the Mistassini Cree Hunters*, Social and Economic Studies, no. 23 (St. John's, Newfoundland: Institute of Social and Economic Research, Memorial University of Newfoundland, 1979), 137–38, 151; Frank G. Speck, *Naskapi: The Savage Hunters of the Labrador Peninsula* (Norman: University of Oklahoma Press, 1935), 76–81. The pattern of communication and dependence on animal spirits and supernaturals found among modern eastern subarctic groups is evident as

well in historical sources; see *Jesuit Relations* 6:159, 213, 215; 7:163. See also Martin, *Keepers of the Game*, 119–22; and Calvin Martin, "Subarctic Indians and Wildlife," in *Old Trails and New Directions: Papers of the Third North American Fur Trade Conference*, ed. Carol M. Judd and Arthur J. Ray (Toronto: University of Toronto Press, 1979), 73–81. Landes (*Ojibwa Religion*, 35) was told by her informants that without the aid of supernatural guardians men were "empty, fearful, and cowardly" for life. Hallowell (*Culture and Experience*, 360–61) was struck by the urgency with which Saulteaux Ojibwa men sought to establish spiritual alliances: "It was absolutely imperative that males, rather than females, seek out and obtain superhuman aid. Women might obtain such help; men could not get along without it." Historical sources also document men's need for supernatural aid; see *Jesuit Relations* 6:213, 7:61; Chrestien Le Clercq, *New Relation of Gaspesia: With the Customs and Religion of the Gaspesian Indians* (1691), trans. and ed. William F. Ganong (Toronto: Champlain Society, 1910; reprinted New York: Greenwood Press, 1968), 225–29.

11. Edward S. Rogers and James G. E. Smith, "Environment and Culture in the Shield and Mackenzie Borderlands," in Helm, *Subarctic*, 130–45; Robert E. Ritzenthaler, "Southwestern Chippewa," in *Handbook of North American Indians*, vol. 15: *Northeast*, ed. Bruce G. Trigger (Washington, D.C.: Smithsonian Institution, 1978), 743–59.

12. Hallowell, *Culture and Experience*, 92, 178, 205; Landes, *Ojibwa Woman*, 18; Tanner, *Bringing Home Animals*, 176–77.

13. Ritzenthaler, "Southwestern Chippewa"; Nicolas Denys, *The Description and Natural History of the Coasts of North America (Acadia)* (1672), trans. and ed. William F. Ganong (Toronto: Champlain Society, 1908; reprinted New York: Greenwood Press, 1968), 422; *Jesuit Relations* 16:83.

14. *Jesuit Relations* 6:233. Le Clercq (*New Relation*, 119) also noted that women were in charge of distributing meat.

15. Leacock, "Women's Status in Egalitarian Society"; Tanner, *Bringing Home Animals*, 176–77.

16. Denys, *Description and Natural History*, 404; *Jesuit Relations* 16:67. See also Marc Lescarbot, *Nova Francia, a Description of Acadia* (1606) (New York: Harper, 1928), 153. The concept of women's childbearing activities as a source of status and power within the family is examined in Patricia Draper, "!Kung Women: Contrasts in Sexual Egalitarianism in Foraging and Sedentary Contexts," in *Toward an Anthropology of Women*, ed. Rayna R. Reiter (New York: Monthly Review Press, 1975), 77–109; and Mary C. Wright, "Economic Development and Native American Women in the Early Nineteenth Century,"

American Quarterly 33 (1981): 525–36. See also Leacock, "Women's Status in Egalitarian Society"; *Jesuit Relations* 3:109; Sieur de Diereville, *Relation of the Voyage to Port Royal in Acadia of New France* (1708), trans. Mrs. Clarence Webster, ed. John Clarence Webster (Toronto: Champlain Society, 1933), 148; Ellice Becker Gonzalez, "The Changing Economic Roles for Micmac Men and Women: An Ethnohistorical Analysis" (Ph.D. diss., State University of New York at Stony Brook, 1979), 37. For further descriptions of women's responsibilities, see *Jesuit Relations* 2:77, 3:247; Lescarbot, *Nova Francia*, 253; Le Clercq, *New Relation*, 102, 162; Gonzalez, "Changing Economic Roles," 47; Tanner, *Bringing Home Animals*, 176, 178–80.

17. *Jesuit Relations* 9:113; see also 9:119, 14:183. Landes, *Ojibwa Religion*, 40–41, and *Ojibwa Woman*, 163, describes twentieth-century women's shamanistic activities.

18. Le Clercq, *New Relation*, 293–94. See also *Jesuit Relations* 6:191, 219, 279; 9:121. The rear limbs of beaver, bear, and caribou are also women's special foods among some twentieth-century Cree and Montagnais-Naskapi bands; see Tanner, *Bringing Home Animals*, 161–62; Speck, *Naskapi*, 96; Philip K. Bock, "Micmac," in Trigger, *Northeast*, 109–22.

19. Women's spiritual potency is recounted in *Jesuit Relations* 9:123, 3:105; Denys, *Description and Natural History*, 409–10; Diereville, *Relation of the Voyage to Port Royal*, 162; Diamond Jenness, *The Ojibwa Indians of Parry Island: Their Social and Religious Life*, Canada Department of Mines, National Museum of Canada, Bulletin no. 78, Anthropological Series, no. 17 (Ottawa: J. O. Patenuade, 1935), 96–97; Landes, *Ojibwa Religion*, 40–41.

20. See, for example, Christopher Vecsey, *Traditional Ojibwa Religion and Its Historical Changes* (Philadelphia: American Philosophical Society, 1983), 45. The following studies, however, indicate that the impact of contact at times was quite severe: Leacock, "Montagnais Women"; Cornelius J. Jaenen, *Friend and Foe: Aspects of French-Amerindian Cultural Contact in the Sixteenth and Seventeenth Centuries* (New York: Columbia University Press, 1976); Cornelius J. Jaenen, "Conceptual Frameworks for French Views of America and Amerindians," *French Colonial Studies* 2 (1978): 1–22; also Alfred Goldsworthy Bailey, *The Conflict of European and Eastern Algonkian Cultures, 1504–1700: A Study in Canadian Civilization*, New Brunswick Museum Monographic Series, no. 2 (St. John, 1937; reprinted Toronto: University of Toronto Press, 1979), 114.

21. See Elman R. Service, *Primitive Social Organization: An Evolutionary Perspective* (New York: Random House, 1962), 108–9, for an

explanation of band structure; and Leacock, "Women's Status in Egalitarian Society."

22. Bruce G. Trigger, *The Children of Aataentsic: A History of the Huron People to 1660*, 2 vols. (Montreal: McGill-Queen's University Press, 1976), examines precontact trade patterns along the St. Lawrence.

23. Denys, *Description and Natural History*, 426; also 403; Gonzalez, "Changing Economic Roles," 84–89.

24. *Jesuit Relations* 1:173; also 3:95; Bailey, *Conflict*, 6.

25. *Jesuit Relations* 5:171.

26. Ibid., 1:87.

27. Ibid., 16:33; W. J. Eccles, *The Canadian Frontier, 1534–1760* (New York: Holt, Rinehart & Winston, 1969), 32.

28. Louis Armand de Lom d'Arce, baron de Lahontan, *New Voyages to North America* (1703), ed. Reuben Gold Thwaites (New York: Burt Franklin, 1905; reprinted New York: Lenox Hill, 1970), 2:420.

29. *Jesuit Relations*, intro., 1:xxxi–xxxiii.

30. Ibid., 4:207.

31. Denys, *Description and Natural History*, 187; also Gonzalez, "Changing Economic Roles," 90; Eleanor Leacock, "The Montagnais 'Hunting Territory' and the Fur Trade," *American Anthropological Memoirs*, no. 78 (Menasha, Wis.: American Anthropological Association, 1954), 7, 26; Harold A. Innis, *The Fur Trade in Canada: An Introduction to Canadian Economic History*, rev. ed. (Toronto: University of Toronto Press, 1956), 16.

32. *Jesuit Relations* 3:69.

33. Ibid., 4:207.

34. Ibid., 5:25.

35. Ibid., 3:77.

36. Richard J. Perry, "The Fur Trade and the Status of Women in the Western Subarctic," *Ethnohistory* 26, no. 4 (1979): 363–75, suggests that changing productive patterns among Athabascans of the western subarctic decreased women's social, economic, and personal authority and lowered their status. Judith Brown, "Iroquois Women: An Ethnohistoric Note," in Reiter, *Toward an Anthropology of Women*, 235–51, demonstrates that Iroquois women's high status was related directly to control over their work and its product. Mona Etienne, "Women and Men, Cloth and Colonization: The Transformation of Production-Distribution Relations Among the Baule (Ivory Coast)," in Etienne and Leacock, *Women and Colonization*, 214–38, illustrates a loss of power among contemporary Baule women.

37. Gonzalez, "Changing Economic Roles," 53–57, 99, 105; Wright, "Economic Development," sees coast and seaboard Salish

women as "invisible employees" of the fur trade who worked for their husbands and experienced a noticeable loss in economic power.

38. Calvin Martin, "The Four Lives of a Micmac Copper Pot," *Ethnohistory* 22, no. 2 (1975): 111–33; Innis, *Fur Trade*, 18.

39. *Jesuit Relations* 68:93.

40. Denys, *Description and Natural History*, 405; Gonzalez, "Changing Economic Roles," 46. Iron hatchets were another item that, while making firewood collection easier for women, also made frequent moves more feasible.

41. *Jesuit Relations* 6:273; also Marc Lescarbot, *The History of New France* (1618), trans. by W. L. Grant, 3 vols. (Toronto: The Champlain Society, 1907–1914; reprinted Greenwood Press, 1968), 1:310, 320.

42. Denys, *Description and Natural History*, 447–49; Gonzalez, "Changing Economic Roles," 53–58, 95–99. Harold Hickerson, "The Chippewa of the Upper Great Lakes: A Study in Sociopolitical Change," in *North American Indians in Historical Perspective*, ed. by Eleanor Burke Leacock and Nancy Oestreich Lurie (New York: Random House, 1971), 186, describes "individualization of the distribution of food" and dependence on European food among Chippewa.

43. Gonzalez, "Changing Economic Roles," 102–3; Perry, "Fur Trade and the Status of Women."

44. *Jesuit Relations* 12:123. See also James P. Ronda, "The European Indian: Jesuit Civilization Planning in New France," *Church History* 41, no. 3 (1972): 385–95.

45. *Jesuit Relations* 3:123; also 1:172; Le Clercq, *New Relation*, 104; Cornelius J. Jaenen, "Amerindian Views of French Culture in the Seventeenth Century," *Canadian Historical Review* 55, no. 3 (1974): 261–91; James Ronda, in " 'We Are Well As We Are': An Indian Critique of Seventeenth-Century Christian Missions," *William and Mary Quarterly* 24, no. 1 (1977): 66–82, maintains that women and men both reacted against the Christian dogma of sin, guilt, damnation, and baptism. Some accepted Christianity, "but whatever their responses, Indian peoples did demonstrate that their traditions were dynamic intellectual systems, capable of change" (67).

46. *Jesuit Relations* 14:205; also Ronda, "European Indian." James Axtell describes Sillery as "the Christian showplace of Laurentian Canada" during its early years (*The Invasion Within: The Contest of Cultures in Colonial North America* [New York: Oxford University Press, 1985], 61).

47. *Jesuit Relations* 14:213–15.

48. Ibid., 16:199; also 57:239, 62:39.

49. Ibid., 18:39–41; also 24:209–13.

50. Ibid., 6:143; also 6:135, 12:141.

51. Ibid., 5:145; also 16:59; 18:137; 20:191.

52. Leacock, "Montagnais Women"; *Jesuit Relations* 14:263.

53. *Jesuit Relations* 32:289.

54. Ibid., 37:43 (Rageuneau), 58:277 (André); see also 62:45. Fr. Jacques Bigot at the Sillery-Abnaki mission commented in 1681 that some Indian women used iron girdles for self-mortification.

55. Ibid., 22:83, 16:61.

56. Ibid., 18:105–7.

57. Louise S. Spindler, *Menomini Women and Culture Change*, American Anthropological Association Memoir no. 91 (Menasha, Wis.: American Anthropological Association, 1962), found that many Menomini women, regardless of their "acculturation" level (including those who were practicing Christians), covertly retained many older concepts of female identity.

58. Le Clercq, *New Relation*, 229.

59. *Jesuit Relations* 56:23–25, 79; 58:89; among Hurons, 55:23. See also Bailey, *Conflict*, 100; Jacqueline Louise Peterson, "The People in Between: Indian-White Marriage and the Genesis of a Metis Society and Culture in the Great Lakes Region, 1680–1830" (Ph.D. diss., University of Illinois at Chicago Circle, 1981). Michelle Zimbalist Rosaldo, "Woman, Culture, and Society: A Theoretical Overview," in *Woman, Culture, and Society*, ed. Michelle Zimbalist Rosaldo and Louise Lamphere (Stanford: Stanford University Press, 1974), 17–42, considers the role of convents in Western culture.

60. Lahontan, *New Voyages* 2:463.

61. *Jesuit Relations* 20:195–97; also Marie de L'Incarnation, *Word from New France: The Selected Letters of Marie de l'Incarnation*, trans. and ed. Joyce Marshall (Toronto: Oxford University Press, 1967), 85–88; Bailey, *Conflict*, 104.

62. *Jesuit Relations* 22:83; also 20:191.

63. Ibid., 22:85.

64. Ibid., 81–85; also 18:155, 22:117–21, 24:47–49, 26:99.

65. Ibid., 54:143, 145.

66. Ibid., 57:269.

67. Ibid., 273.

68. Martin, *Keepers of the Game*, 50–62.

69. *Jesuit Relations* 1:257; also Jaenen, *Friend and Foe*. Edmund S. Morgan, *American Slavery, American Freedom: The Ordeal of Colonial Virginia* (New York: Norton, 1975), 63, discusses the attitudes of European gentlemen toward labor.

70. Carolyn C. Lougee, *Le Paradis des Femmes: Women, Salons, and Social Stratification in Seventeenth-Century France* (Princeton: Princeton University Press, 1976), 209. William V. Bangert, S.J., *A History of the Society of Jesus* (St. Louis: Institute of Jesuit Sources, 1972).

71. Le Clercq, *New Relation*, 263.

72. *Jesuit Relations* 5:181–83.

73. Ibid., 18:35, 155; 22:81–85. Leacock, "Montagnais Women."

74. *Jesuit Relations* 50:291; also 6:253; Denys, *Description and Natural History*, 415.

75. *Jesuit Relations* 24:47.

76. Pierre Boucher, *True and Genuine Description of New France, Commonly Called Canada, and of the Manners and Customs and Productions of That Country* (1664), translated by Edward Louis Montizambert (Montreal: George E. Desbarats, 1883), 56.

77. *Jesuit Relations* 16:41; also 5:111, 7:143; Le Clercq, *New Relation*, 242; Denys, *Description and Natural History*, 411.

78. *Jesuit Relations* 14:263.

79. Ibid., 6:255.

80. Ibid., 22:81–85; also 5:181, 6:255, 18:155, 22:117–21, 24:47–49, 26:99.

81. Ibid., 12:165 (quote), 55:111, 56:215; see also Leacock, "Montagnais Women," on Jesuit attempts to institute monogamy and marital fidelity.

82. *Jesuit Relations* 25:109.

83. Ibid., 55:129–31; also 57:217.

84. *Jesuit Relations* 36:197, 201; 16:33.

85. Eleanor Leacock, "Seventeenth-Century Montagnais Social Relations and Values," in Helm, *Subarctic*, 190–95. For analyses of the impact of the public-private division on women's status, see Karen Sacks, "Engels Revisited: Women, the Organization of Production, and Private Property," in Reiter, *Toward an Anthropology of Women*, 211–34; and Peggy R. Sanday, "Female Status in the Public Domain," in Rosaldo and Lamphere, *Woman, Culture, and Society*, 189–206.

86. *Jesuit Relations* 5:179; 6:255; 18:135, 155; 22:81–85. On the development of the independent nuclear family following dependence on the fur trade, see Leacock, "Women's Status in Egalitarian Society"; Edward S. Rogers, "The Mistassini Cree," in *Hunters and Gatherers Today: A Socioeconomic Study of Eleven Such Cultures in the Twentieth Century*, ed. M. G. Bicchiere (New York: Holt, Rinehart & Winston, 1972), 133; and Eleanor Leacock, "The Montagnais-Naskapi Band," in *Contributions to Anthropology: Band Societies*, ed. David Damas, National Museum of Canada, Bulletin no. 228, An-

thropological Series, no. 84 (Ottawa: The Queen's Printer, 1969), 1–17.

87. *Jesuit Relations* 26:113–15, 29:107; Leacock, "Montagnais 'Hunting Territory' "; and Eleanor Leacock, "Matrilocality in a Simple Hunting Economy (Montagnais-Naskapi)," *Southwestern Journal of Anthropology* 11, no. 1 (1955): 31–47.

88. *Jesuit Relations* 6:297–99, 20:187–89, 24:209, 29:163, 37:59.

89. Ibid., 2:77; also 3:133, 14:233, 16:37.

90. Martin, *Keepers of the Game*, 53–65.

91. Leacock, "Montagnais-Naskapi Band" and "Matrilocality"; Charles A. Bishop and Shepard Krech III, "Matriorganization: The Basis of Aboriginal Subarctic Social Organization," *Arctic Anthropology* 17, no. 2 (1980): 34–45; *Jesuit Relations* 30:169.

CHAPTER 2

1. J. H. Kennedy, *Jesuit and Savage in New France* (New Haven: Yale University Press, 1950), 44–46; Axtell, *The Invasion Within*, 65–70.

2. Kennedy, *Jesuit and Savage*, 48–50; Lucien Campeau, S.J., "Roman Catholic Missions in New France," in *Handbook of North American Indians*, vol. 4: *History of Indian-White Relations*, ed. Wilcomb E. Washburn (Washington, D.C.: Smithsonian Institution, 1988), 464–71; *Jesuit Relations* 68:79; Vecsey, *Traditional Ojibwa Religion*, 45.

3. Jacqueline Peterson, "Ethnogenesis: The Settlement and Growth of a 'New People' in the Great Lakes Region, 1702–1815," in *An Anthology of Western Great Lakes Indian History*, ed. Donald L. Fixico (Milwaukee: American Indian Studies, University of Wisconsin, 1987), 111–77.

4. Campeau, "Roman Catholic Missions"; John Boatman, "Historical Overview of the Wisconsin Area: From Early Years to the French, British, and Americans," in Fixico, *Anthology of Western Great Lakes Indian History*, 13–68; Mary Doris Mulvey, O.P., *French Catholic Missionaries in the Present United States, 1604–1791*, Catholic University of America Studies in Church History, no. 23 (Washington, D.C.: Catholic University, 1936), 41–54; Sr. Mary Aquinas Norton, *Catholic Missionary Activities in the Northwest, 1818–1864* (Washington, D.C.: Catholic University, 1930), 6; Vecsey, *Traditional Ojibwa Religion*, 27.

5. Kennedy, *Jesuit and Savage*, 53; John Dawson Gilmary Shea, *History of the Catholic Missions Among the Indian Tribes of the United States, 1529–1854* (New York: E. Dunnigan, 1855), 619.

6. Methodists (later extremely active in missions to Indians both through English and American mission societies) did not arrive in the colonies until 1768, and they waited until the 1790s to begin systematic proselytizing; see Charles L. Chaney, *The Birth of Missions in America* (South Pasadena, Calif.: William Carey Library, 1976), 98–114. The New England Company had missionaries to Indians for one hundred years (70–71).

7. Jack H. Steinbring, "Saulteaux of Lake Winnipeg," in Helm, *Subarctic*, 244–55; Charles A. Bishop, *The Northern Ojibwa and the Fur Trade: An Historical and Ecological Study* (Montreal: Holt, Rinehart & Winston, 1974), 308–21; Vecsey, *Traditional Ojibwa Religion*, 12–15.

8. James McKenzie, "The King's Posts and Journal of a Canoe Jaunt Through the King's Domains, 1808: The Saguenay and the Labrador Coast," in *Les bourgeois de la Compagnie du Nord-Ouest: Récits de voyages, Lettres et Rapports Inedits Relatifs au Nord-Ouest Canadien*, ed. L. R. Masson (Quebec: A. Cote, 1889–90; reprinted New York: Antiquarian Press, 1960), 2:412–13.

9. Bishop, *Northern Ojibwa and the Fur Trade*, 10–12, 236–45; Rande S. Aaronson, "Workers and Wages in the Canadian Fur Trade, 1773–1775," unpublished paper.

10. Duncan Cameron, "The Nipigon Country, 1804, with Extracts from His Journal," in Masson, *Les bourgeois de la Compagnie du Nord-Ouest* 2:295–96; see also Peter Grant, "The Sauteux Indians About 1804," in ibid., 2:325, on Indians cheating traders.

11. Cameron, "Nipigon Country," 2:296; Bishop, *Northern Ojibwa and the Fur Trade*, 11–12, 245–56.

12. Charles McKenzie, Hudson's Bay Company Archives B107/a/8; cited in Bishop, *Northern Ojibwa and the Fur Trade*, 283.

13. Bishop, *Northern Ojibwa and the Fur Trade*, 39, 265; David Thompson, *David Thompson's Narrative, of His Explorations in Western America, 1784–1812*, ed. J. B. Tyrrell (Toronto: Champlain Society, 1916; reprinted New York: Greenwood Press, 1968), 70.

14. George Keith, "Letters to Mr. Roderic McKenzie, 1807–1817," in Masson, *Les bourgeois de la Compagnie du Nord-Ouest* 2:61–132; Willard Ferdinand Wentzel, "Letters to the Hon. Roderic McKenzie, 1807–1824," in ibid., 1:67–153; Edward Umfreville, *The Present State of Hudson's Bay, Containing a Full Description of That Settlement and the Adjacent Country and Likewise of the Fur Trade, with Hints for Its Improvement* (London, 1790), 66–67.

15. Sylvia Van Kirk, *"Many Tender Ties": Women in Fur-Trade Society, 1670–1870* (Winnipeg: Watson & Dwyer, 1980), 9–27.

16. Henry Kelsey, *The Kelsey Papers* (Ottawa: Public Archives of Canada and Public Record Office of Northern Ireland, 1929), 21. For

more on Kelsey, see K. G. Davies, "Henry Kelsey," *Dictionary of Canadian Biography*, ed. Francess G. Halpenny (Toronto: University of Toronto Press, 1966–90), 2:307–15.

17. P. Grant, "Sauteux Indians," 2:321. Xanthippes was married to Socrates and noted for her sharp tongue and vehement manner.

18. Philip Turnor, *Journals of Samuel Hearne and Philip Turnor*, ed. J. B. Tyrrell (Toronto: Champlain Society, 1934), 273.

19. John McDonnell, "Some Account of the Red River (About 1797), with Extracts from His Journal, 1793–1795," in Masson, *Les bourgeois de la Compagnie du Nord-Ouest* 1:278. Evidence of women's authority and social value applied as well to groups such as the Dogribs, Beaver, and Slaves—Athapaskan-speaking groups in the western subarctic whose men, since the inception of the fur trade, apparently held women in decreasing regard. Willard Ferdinand Wentzel, a Norwegian employed by the North West Company and married to a Montagnais woman, observed in a letter to Roderic McKenzie in 1807 that there appeared to be few women among the Beaver Indians at the Forks area of the Mackenzie River, a fact that he attributed to female infanticide. "The only reason they five for this barbarous custom," he explained, "is that it is a great deal of trouble to bring up girls, and that women are only an encumbrance, useless in time of war and exceedingly voracious in time of want." Yet in the same letter he went on to say that "their husbands are very kind to them, their only business being to make the men's clothes and their own, while the men's work is to chop wood, strike fire, make the campment, hunt, &c, &c." (Wentzel, "Letters," 1:86–87). McKenzie also received a letter that same year from George Keith, who spent most of his career in the western subarctic and was a chief factor for the Hudson's Bay Company after the 1821 merger. Keith described the life of Beaver women in glowing terms: "The women are indulged with everything attainable, without being subjected to any brutal treatment or hard menial labour, as many other tribes in this country." Several years later his views had not changed: "The women seldom prepare the lodge in winter, or go for wood unless the husband is absent and the men perform all the hard labours, so indulgent they are to the women." Dogrib women from Filthy Lake impressed Keith as well, about whom he noted that they "are gently treated and have considerable influence over the men" (Keith, "Letters," 2:70, 115).

20. Thompson, *Narrative*, xv, xxv, xlv, 82, 246 (quote). For full biographical information on Thompson, see John Nicks, "David Thompson," in Halpenny, *Dictionary of Canadian Biography* 8:878–84.

21. Thompson, *Narrative*, 82.

22. Ibid., 164.

23. Ibid., 92.

24. Ibid.

25. Ibid., 88, 108; see also Frances Densmore, *Chippewa Customs*, Smithsonian Institution, Bureau of American Ethnology, Bulletin no. 86 (Washington, D.C.: Government Printing Office, 1929), 29.

26. For more on Cameron, see Jennifer S. H. Brown, "Duncan Cameron," in Halpenny, *Dictionary of Canadian Biography* 7:137–39.

27. Cameron, "Nipigon Country," 2:257.

28. Ruth Schwartz Cowan, *More Work for Mother: The Ironies of Household Technology, from the Open Hearth to the Microwave* (New York: Basic Books, 1983), chaps. 2–3.

29. Cameron, "Nipigon Country," 2:257, 258.

30. Ibid., 262–63.

31. James Isham, *James Isham's Observations on Hudsons Bay, 1743; and Notes and Observations on a Book Entitled "A Voyage to Hudsons Bay in the Dobbs Galley, 1749,"* ed. E. E. Rich (Toronto: Champlain Society, 1949), 98.

32. Cameron, "Nipigon Country," 2:263. See also Martin, *Keepers of the Game*, 64; *Jesuit Relations* 3:105–9.

33. John Tanner, *Narrative of the Captivity and Adventures of John Tanner (U.S. Interpreter at the Sault de Ste. Marie) During Thirty Years Residence Among the Indians in the Interior of North America*, ed. Edwin James (New York: G. & C. & H. Carvil, 1830), 47. See also Charles Chaboillez, "Journal of Charles Jean Baptiste Chaboillez, 1797–1798," ed. Harold Hickerson, *Ethnohistory* 6, no. 3 (1959): 265–316; 6, no. 4 (1959): 363–427.

34. Speck, *Naskapi*, 94, 115, 180–83; A. Tanner, *Bringing Home Animals*, 125–26, 136–37, 140.

35. J. Tanner, *Narrative*, 67.

36. Henry Schoolcraft, *The Indian in His Wigwam, or Characteristics of the Red Race of America* (Buffalo, 1848), 169–73, cited in Priscilla K. Buffalohead, "Farmers, Warriors, Traders: A Fresh Look at Ojibway Women," *Minnesota History* 48 (Summer 1983): 236–44.

37. Thompson, *Narrative*, 246.

38. Selwyn Dewdney, *The Sacred Scrolls of the Southern Ojibwa* (Toronto: University of Toronto Press, 1975), 163–67; Ritzenthaler, "Southwestern Chippewa"; Martin, *Keepers of the Game*, 84–85; Harold Hickerson, "Notes on the Post-Contact Origin of the Midewiwin," *Ethnohistory* 9 (1962): 406.

39. P. Grant, "Sauteux Indians," 356.

40. Vecsey, *Traditional Ojibwa Religion*, 156, 182–83.

41. P. Grant, "The Sauteux Indians," 361.

42. Landes, *Ojibwa Religion*, 89.

43. Ibid., 91; Densmore, *Chippewa Customs*, 87.

44. J. Tanner, *Narrative*, passim.

45. Thompson, *Narrative*, 255; Vecsey, *Traditional Ojibwa Religion*, 141.

46. J. Tanner, *Narrative*, 135.

47. Isham, *Observations*, 100.

48. Cameron, "Nipigon Country," 2:250; Morton I. Teicher, *Windigo Psychosis: A Study of a Relationship Between Belief and Behavior Among the Indians of Northeastern Canada* (New York: AMS Press, 1985).

49. Vivian J. Rohrl, "A Nutritional Factor in Windigo Psychosis," *American Anthropologist* 72 (1970): 97–101, suggests that the remedy of ingesting tallow was nutritionally based, to counteract a dietary deficiency in ascorbic acid (of which bear fat has a high content), which possibly caused the psychosis. This hypothesis has been challenged by Jennifer S. H. Brown, "The Cure and Feeding of Windigos: A Critique," *American Anthropologist* 73 (1971): 19–22.

50. George Nelson, *"The Orders of the Dreamed": George Nelson on Cree and Northern Ojibwa Religion and Myth*, ed. Jennifer S. H. Brown and Robert Brightman, Manitoba Studies in History, vol. 3 (St. Paul: Minnesota Historical Society, 1988), 170. See also Steinbring, "Saulteaux," 253.

51. Cameron, "Nipigon Country," 2:250; also Nelson, *"Orders of the Dreamed,"* 94.

52. Nelson, *"Orders of the Dreamed,"* 94.

53. Thompson, *Narrative*, 259–60.

54. Ruth Landes, "The Abnormal Among the Ojibwa Indians," *Journal of Abnormal and Social Psychology* 33 (1938): 14–33; Seymour Parker, "The Wiitiko Psychosis in the Context of Ojibwa Personality and Culture," *American Anthropologist* 62 (1960): 603–23, contends that the syndrome is primarily male and suggests that the personality development and socialization of Ojibwa males, which emphasize success, might provoke psychosis when an individual fails in hunting. Teicher's study of seventy reported psychosis cases, however, showed a four-to-three ratio between males and females ("Windigo Psychosis"). See also Raymond D. Fogelson, "Psychological Theories of Windigo 'Psychosis' and a Preliminary Application of a Models Approach," in *Context and Meaning in Cultural Anthropology*, ed. Melford E. Spiro (New York: Free Press, 1965), 74–99.

55. Early references to windigos do not mention cannibalism; it is debatable whether the concept developed after European contact or if observers did not understand the descriptions they were given by Indians. For more information, see Jennifer S. H. Brown and Robert Brightman, "Northern Algonquian Religious and Mythic Themes and Personages: Context and Comparisons," in Nelson, *Orders of the Dreamed*," 161. For an analysis of a similar phenomenon, stress-related witch hunting in Salem, see Paul Boyer and Stephen Nissenbaum, *Salem Possessed: The Social Origins of Witchcraft* (Cambridge, Mass.: Harvard University Press, 1974).

CHAPTER 3

1. Sherman Hall to Laura D. Hall, 20 February 1833, Sherman Hall Papers (hereafter cited as SH), Minnesota Historical Society.

2. The British-based New England Company supported missionaries to native communities from the 1640s on. Until the American Revolution forced the English to leave the colonies, the Church of England's Society for the Propagation of the Gospel in Foreign Parts accepted Indians into their schools in an effort to compete with the Presbyterians and Congregationalists for adherents. David Brainerd was notable for his activities in Stockbridge, as were the Mayhews in Martha's Vineyard; see Chaney, *Birth of Missions*, 70–71, 104–10; Ernest Hawkins, *Historical Notices of the Missions of the Church of England in the North American Colonies, previous to the Independence of the United States: Chiefly from the M. S. Documents of the Society for the Propagation of the Gospel in Foreign Parts* (London: B. Fellowes, 1845), 342; Henry Warner Bowden, *American Indians and Christian Missions: Studies in Conflict* (Chicago: University of Chicago Press, 1981), 136; William G. McLoughlin, Jr., *Modern Revivalism: Charles Grandison Finney to Billy Graham* (New York: Ronald Press, 1959), 23–24, 120–21; Timothy L. Smith, *Revivalism and Social Reform: American Protestantism on the Eve of the Civil War* (Baltimore: Johns Hopkins University Press, 1980), 58–62; John Webster Grant, *Moon of Wintertime: Missionaries and the Indians of Canada in Encounter Since 1534* (Toronto: University of Toronto Press, 1984), 72–75.

3. Chaney, *Birth of Missions*, 98, 154; Wade Crawford Barclay, *History of Methodist Missions*. Vol. 1: *Early American Methodism, 1769–1844* (New York: Board of Missions and Church Extension of the Methodist Church, 1949–50), 1:164–66; William R. Hutchison, *Errand to the World: American Protestant Thought and Foreign Missions* (Chicago: University of Chicago Press, 1987), 46, 58.

4. Norton, *Catholic Missionary Activities*, 44; A. G. Morice, *History of the Catholic Church in Western Canada, from Lake Superior to the Pacific (1659–1895)*, 2 vols. (Toronto: Musson, 1910), 1:132–36. The mission removed to the Red River (Fort Garry/Winnipeg) site. By 1791, fewer than six Protestant missionaries were known to be working in Upper Canada, a territory of seven hundred thousand square miles; see Barclay, *Early American Methodism*, 180.

5. [Stephen H. Long], *Narrative of an Expedition to the Source of St. Peter's River, Lake Winnepeek, Lake of the Woods, &c. Performed in the Years 1823, by Order of the Hon. J. C. Calhoun, Secretary of War, Under the Command of Stephen H. Long, U.S.A.* (1824), ed. William H. Keating (Minneapolis: Ross & Haines, 1959), 39.

6. Elliot Coues, ed., *New Light on the Early History of the Greater Northwest: The Manuscript Journals of Alexander Henry and of David Thompson*, 2 vols. (Minneapolis: Ross & Haines, 1965), 1:239–40. For more on Henry, see Barry M. Gough, "Alexander Henry," in Halpenny, *Dictionary of Canadian Biography* 5:418–19.

7. Long, *Narrative*, 69–70.

8. Barclay, *Early American Methodism*, 202; Walter N. Vernon and Ruth M. Vernon, "Indian Missions of North America," in *Encyclopedia of World Methodism*, ed. Nolan B. Harmon (Nashville: United Methodist Publishing House, 1974), 1211; Laura L. Peers, "Rich Man, Poor Man, Beggarman, Chief: Saulteaux in the Red River Settlement," in *Papers of the Eighteenth Algonquian Conference*, ed. William Cowan (Ottawa: Carleton University Press, 1987), 261–70.

9. John West, *The Substance of a Journal During a Residence at the Red River Colony* (London: Seeley, 1824; reprinted New York: Johnson Reprint, 1966), v.

10. Bishop, *Northern Ojibwa and the Fur Trade*, 348; Arthur J. Ray, *Indians in the Fur Trade: Their Role as Trappers, Hunters, and Middlemen in the Lands Southwest of Hudson Bay, 1660–1870* (Toronto: University of Toronto Press, 1974), 199–204; Edward S. Rogers, "Cultural Adaptations: The Northern Ojibwa of the Boreal Forest, 1670–1890," in *Boreal Forest Adaptations: The Northern Algonkians*, ed. A. Theodore Steegmann, Jr. (New York: Plenum Press, 1983), 85–142. While Bishop and Ray consider the period of fur trade dependency to have begun with the amalgamation of the HBC and the North West Company, Paul C. Thistle, *Indian-European Trade Relations in the Lower Saskatchewan River Region to 1840* (Winnipeg: University of Manitoba Press, 1986), maintains that Cree followed their own "Zen road to affluence," independent of European influence until the introduction of missionaries and government agents in the 1840s.

11. James Dixon, *Personal Narrative of a Tour Through a Part of the United States and Canada: With Notices of the History and Institutions of Methodism in America* (New York: Lane & Scott, 1849), pp. 422–24; Vernon and Vernon, "Indian Missions"; Donald B. Smith, *Sacred Feathers: The Reverend Peter Jones (Kahkewaquonaby) and the Mississauga Indians* (Toronto: University of Toronto Press, 1987), 73–74.

12. G. G. Findlay and W. W. Holdsworth, *The History of the Wesleyan Methodist Missionary Society*, 5 vols. (London: Epworth, 1821), 1:387.

13. Extract from Meeting of General Committee, Wesleyan Missionary Society, 11 May 1831, Wesleyan Methodist Missionary Society Archives, London–North American Correspondence (microfiche), United Methodist Archives and History Center, Madison, N.J. (hereafter cited as WMMS), Box 100, 1837/38, 10C; Rev. Alexander Sutherland, "The Methodist Church in Relation to Missions," in *Centennial of Canadian Methodism* (Toronto: William Briggs, 1891), 253–60; Barclay, *Early American Methodism*, 97; D. A. Bacon, comp., "Wesleyan Methodist Church (Great Britain)," Vol. 1: "Foreign Missions: America. The British Dominions in North America. Correspondence 1791–1893." 4 vols., United Methodist Archives and History Center, Madison, N.J. (1973), 1:14–16; Findlay and Holdsworth, *History* 1:423–27.

14. Jurisdictional conflict raged again in 1839, with the Canada Conference insisting that the British had "no right to interfere" in Canadian missions; see Minutes of Canada Conference, 12 June 1839, Hamilton, Ont., WMMS Box 101, 1839/40, 11C; Stinson to Alder, 1 July 1839, WMMS, ibid. At one point, the Canadians—or Ryersonians, as they called themselves—locked the Salt Springs converts out of the chapel when the Mohawks announced their intention of remaining loyal to the British Wesleyans; see Moses Walker, William Hess, et al. to J. Stinson, 30 January 1841, WMMS Box 102, 1841/42, 12C. For a discussion of missionary politics, see Elizabeth Graham, *Medicine Man to Missionary: Missionaries as Agents of Change Among the Indians of Southern Ontario, 1784–1867* (Toronto: Peter Martin, 1975), 23, 27, 47.

15. J. T. [Stinson], Secretary, to Rev. William Case, 13 June 1831, WMMS Box 100, 1837/38, 10C.

16. Turner to James, 7 March 1833, WMMS Box 98, 1833/34, 8C.

17. Turner to Alder, 15 January 1834, WMMS Box 98, 1833/34, 8C.

18. Stinson to Alder, 18 February, 2 April 1835, WMMS Box 99, 1835/36, 9C.

19. *Christian Advocate and Journal*, 4 January 1828, 70; and *Methodist Missionary Notices*, 15 December 1840; both cited in Graham, *Medicine Man to Missionary*, 53.

20. Stinson to Alder, 4 July 1838, WMMS Box 100, 1837/38, 10C; 2 April 1835, WMMS, Box 99, 1835/36, 9C; Evans to Rev. John Beecham, 1 September 1835, WMMS Box 99, 1835/36, 9C.

21. Jones to Rev. John Beecham, 16 February 1836, WMMS Box 99, 1835/36, 9C.

22. Ibid.

23. Evans to Stinson, 4 August 1838, in James Evans, "Letters of Rev. James Evans, Methodist Missionary, Written During His Journey to and Residence in the Lake Superior Region, 1838–39," ed. Fred Landon, *Ontario History* 28 (1932): 54.

24. Evans to Mrs. Evans, 2 October 1838, in ibid., 61.

25. Ibid.

26. Stinson to Alder, 17 June 1835, WMMS Box 99, 1835/36, 9C.

27. Evans to Stinson, 31 December 1840, WMMS Box 101, 1839/40, 11C.

28. R. Alder to Lord Glenely, Secretary of State for Colonies, December 1837, WMMS Box 100, 1837/38, 10C.

29. Ibid.

30. John Sunday to Alder, 7 April 1841, WMMS Box 102, 1841/42, 12C. For a discussion of mission boarding school routines, see Robert F. Berkhofer, Jr., *Salvation and the Savage: An Analysis of Protestant Missions and American Indian Response, 1787–1862* (Lexington: University of Kentucky Press, 1965), 37–38.

31. Enoch Wood to Alder, 19 March 1848, WMMS Box 104, 1846/48, 14C(2); W. Case to Alder, 2 April 1849, WMMS Box 105, 1849/51, 15C.

32. Alder to Glenely, December 1837, WMMS Box 100, 1837–38, 10C.

33. Peter Jacobs, *Journal of the Reverend Peter Jacobs, Indian Wesleyan Missionary, from Rice Lake to the Hudson's Bay Territory, and Returning. Commencing May, 1852. With a Brief Account of His Life and a Short History of the Wesleyan Mission in That Country* (New York: Printed by the author, 1857), 3–5.

34. Isham, *Observations*, xxviii–xxix.

35. West, *Substance of a Journal*, 13.

36. Norman James Williams, "Abishabis the Cree," *Studies in Religion/Sciences religieuses* 9, no. 2 (1980): 217–45; E. P. Thompson, *The Making of the English Working Class* (New York: Vintage Books, 1966), chap. 11.

37. John McLean, *James Evans: Inventor of the Syllabic System of the Cree Language* (Toronto: Methodist Mission Room, 1890), 191.

38. Findlay and Holdsworth, *History* 1:466–67.

39. George Barnley [to the Secretaries of the Wesleyan Missionary Society], 23 February 1846, WMMS Box 104, 1846/48, 14G. Barnley, in fact, came into open conflict with the post factor over the housing problem; see J. Grant, *Moon of Wintertime*, 106–7, on the relationship between the HBC and the WMMS.

40. Ephraim Evans to Enoch Wood, 11 April 1859, WMMS Box 108, 1858/63, 18C(1). Although Ephraim Evans was writing from a later mission than that of his brother, his guidelines fit any of the WMMS missions.

41. Barbara Welter, "She Hath Done What She Could: Protestant Women's Missionary Careers in Nineteenth-Century America," *American Quarterly* 30 (1978): 624–638; Barbara Welter, "The Cult of True Womanhood: 1820–1860," *American Quarterly* 18 (1966): 151–74.

42. Barnley [to the Secretaries of the Wesleyan Missionary Society], 20 January 1846, WMMS Box 104, 1846/48, 14G; Steinhauer to Mrs. E. Hoole, 6 May 1861, WMMS Box 108, 1858/63, 18G. For biographical information on Eliza Jones, see Smith, *Sacred Feathers*, 130–49; Elizabeth Muir, "The Bark School House: Methodist Episcopal Missionary Women in Upper Canada, 1827–1833," in *Canadian Protestant and Catholic Missions, 1820s–1960s: Historical Essays in Honour of John Webster Grant*, ed. John S. Moir and C. T. McIntire (New York: Peter Lang, 1988), 23–74.

43. Sinclair to Mrs. Elijah Hoole, 16 December 1867, WMMS Box 109, 1864/67, 19G.

44. McLean, *James Evans*, 166–67; George Barnley [to the Secretaries of the Wesleyan Missionary Society?], 23 February 1846, WMMS Box 104, 1846/48, 14G.

45. Hurlburt to Alder, 9 October 1843, WMMS Box 103, 1843/44, 13G.

46. Hurlburt to Robert Alder, 11 January 1841, WMMS Box 102, 1841/42, 12I.

47. Steinhauer to Evans, 7 December 1840, WMMS Box 101, 1839/40, 11G.

48. Jacobs to the Secretaries of the Wesleyan Missionary Society, 4 May 1841, WMMS Box 102, 1841/42, 12I. See also William Mason to the Secretaries, 9 June 1841, WMMS Box 102, 1841/42, 12I.

49. Jacobs to the Secretaries of the Wesleyan Missionary Society, 21 July 1848, WMMS Box 104, 1846/48, 14G.

50. Ibid.

51. Jacobs to the Secretaries of the Wesleyan Missionary Society, 10 December 1849, Box 105, 1849–51, 15G.

52. Ibid.

53. Jacobs to Robert Alder, 6 March 1846, WMMS Box 104, 1846/48, 14G.

54. Jacobs to the Secretaries of the Wesleyan Missionary Society, 21 July 1848, WMMS Box 104, 1846/48, 14G.

55. Jacobs to Robert Alder, 10 February 1850, WMMS Box 419, 1849/51, 15G.

56. Hurlburt to the Secretaries of the Wesleyan Missionary Society, 29 June 1841, WMMS Box 102, 1841/42, 12I.

57. Mason journal, 13 January 1849, WMMS Box 105, 1849/51, 15G.

58. Mason journal, 14 April 1849, WMMS Box 105, 1849/51, 15G; Barnley [to ?], 23 September 1843, WMMS Box 103, 1843/44, 13G. Quote from Mason to the General Secretaries of the Wesleyan Missionary Society, 21 June 1850, WMMS Box 105, 1849/51, 15G. See also McLean, *James Evans*, 166–67; Mason journal, 31 May 1849, WMMS Box 105, 1849/51, 15G.

59. Graham, *Medicine Man to Missionary*, 87–88.

60. William Mason to the Secretaries of the Wesleyan Missionary Society, 9 June 1841, WMMS Box 102, 1841/42, 12I; Jacobs to Sir George Simpson, 2 July 1849, WMMS Box 105, 1849/51, 15G.

61. William Mason to the Secretaries of the Wesleyan Missionary Society, 11 August 1848, WMMS Box 104, 1846/48, 14G. See also George Barnley [to the Secretaries of the Wesleyan Missionary Society], 23 September 1843, WMMS Box 103, 1843/44, 13G. Similar instances of chiefs and shamans renouncing traditional religion are found in the following: Enoch Wood to Robert Alder, 17 February 1851, WMMS Box 105, 1849/51, 15C; Peter Jacobs to the Secretaries of the Wesleyan Missionary Society, 10 December 1849, WMMS Box 105, 1849/51, 15G; William Mason to the Secretaries of the Wesleyan Missionary Society, 19 August 1852, WMMS Box 106, 1852/54, 16G; Thomas Woolsey to Elijah Hoole, 1 March 1862, WMMS Box 108, 1858/63, 18G; Thomas Woolsey to Elijah Hoole, 5 September 1864, WMMS Box 109, 1864/67, 19G.

62. Mason to the Secretaries General of the Wesleyan Missionary Society, [September 1851?], WMMS Box 105, 1849/51, 15G.

63. Evans to Gov. George Simpson, 10 June 1845, WMMS Box 103, 1844/45, 13G; Mason to the Secretaries of the Wesleyan Missionary Society, 11 August 1848, WMMS Box 104, 1846/48, 14G; Mason to

Gov. George Simpson, 20 June 1849, WMMS Box 105, 1849/51, 15G; William Case to Superintendent of Missions, Canada West [Enoch Wood], 31 July 1852, WMMS Box 106, 1852/54, 16C.

64. Mason to the Secretaries of the Wesleyan Missionary Society, 19 August 1852, WMMS Box 106, 1852/54, 16G.

65. Jacobs to the Secretaries of the Wesleyan Missionary Society, 4 May 1841, WMMS Box 102, 1841/42, 12I.

66. James Hope to Mason, April 1852, WMMS Box 106, 1852/54, 16G; Enoch Wood to Robert Alder, 17 February 1851, WMMS Box 105, 1849/51, 15C.

67. John S. Long, "*Manitu*, Power, Books, and *Wiihtikow*: Some Factors in the Adoption of Christianity by Nineteenth-Century Western James Bay Cree," *Native Studies Review* 3, no. 1 (1987): 1–30, accepts earlier historians' claims of speedy conversions among Cree during the nineteenth century. While justly insisting that Indians be viewed as active participants in missionization who used Christianity to meet their own needs, he neglects a consideration of gender in his analysis.

68. Carroll Smith-Rosenberg and Charles Rosenberg, "The Female Animal: Medical and Biological Views of Woman and Her Role in Nineteenth-Century America," *Journal of American History* 60 (1973): 332–56; Barbara Leslie Epstein, *The Politics of Domesticity: Women, Evangelism, and Temperance in Nineteenth-Century America* (Middletown, Conn: Wesleyan University Press, 1981), 85–87.

69. Barbara Ehrenreich and Deirdre English, *Complaints and Disorders: The Sexual Politics of Sickness* (Old Westbury, N.Y.: Feminist Press, 1973), 30–31; Sally Kitch, *Chaste Liberation: Celibacy and Female Cultural Status* (Urbana: University of Illinois Press, 1989), 34, 39; Sarah Stage, *Female Complaints: Lydia Pinkham and the Business of Women's Medicine* (New York: Norton, 1979), 71–72.

70. Philip Greven, *The Protestant Temperament: Patterns of Childrearing, Religious Experience, and the Self in Early America* (New York: Meridian, 1977), 13, 65, 73–74, 124–25; E. P. Thompson, *Making of the English Working Class*, chap. 11.

71. Evans to John Beecham, 29 March 1836, WMMS Box 99, 1835/36, 9C. Peter Jones held similar views; see Jones to John Beecham, 16 February 1836, WMMS Box 99, 1835/36, 9C.

72. Dixon, *Personal Narrative*, 384–85.

73. Secretaries of the Wesleyan Missionary Society to Barnley, 11 March 1840, WMMS Box 101, 1839/40, 11G.

74. Woolsey to Elijah Hoole, 2 March 1862, WMMS Box 108, 1858/63, 18G.

75. Stringfellow to Elijah Hoole, 30 August 1867, WMMS Box 109, 1864/67, 19G; Joseph Stinson to Robert Alder, 15 December 1840, WMMS Box 101, 1839/40, 11C.

76. Benjamin Slight to the Revs. Beecham, Alder, and Hock, Secretaries of the Wesleyan Missionary Society, 30 August 1837, WMMS Box 100, 1837/38, 10C.

77. Stringfellow to Elijah Hoole, 26 December 1866, WMMS Box 109, 1864/67, 19G.

78. William Mason journal, 13 January 1849, WMMS Box 105, 1849/51, 15G; Charles Stringfellow to Elijah Hoole, 26 December 1866, WMMS Box 109, 1864/67, 19G.

79. Barnley [to the Secretaries of the Wesleyan Missionary Society], 23 September 1843, WMMS Box 103, 1843/44, 13G.

80. Ibid.

81. Williams, "Abishabis the Cree." Williams contends that HBC officer James Hargrave at York Factory feared that Abishabis had begun a messianic uprising that threatened the company's security with the Home Guard and with Indians who trapped. Williams sees the movement as an expression of "Manitouism" and a call for a return to an older spiritual and social order. John Webster Grant, "Missionaries and Messiahs in the Northwest," *Studies in Religion/Sciences religieuses*, 9, no. 2 (1980): 125–36, insists, however, that what he terms "unauthorized prophets"—such as Abishabis—represented an effort by Indians to open Christianity to Indians on Indian terms. He suggests that Indians wanted to be colleagues of the missionaries, rather than subjects, and that the prophetic movements were attempts to break into the leadership of Christianity in the northwest. Robert R. Janes and Jane H. Kelley, "Observations on Crisis Cult Activities in the Mackenzie Basin," in *Problems in the Prehistory of the North American Subarctic: The Athapaskan Question*, ed. J. W. Helmer, S. Van Dyke and F. J. Kense (Calgary: Archaeological Association of the University of Calgary, 1977), 153–64, although dealing with a different northwestern culture group, suggest that the prophetic or crisis cults continued precontact shamanistic practices and were in fact an adaptation to stress.

82. Pahtahsekash [Peter Jacobs] to Robert Alder, 13 December 1847, WMMS Box 104, 1846/48, 14G.

83. George Simpson to Robert Alder, 13 August 1846, WMMS Box 104, 1846/48, 14G; William Mason to Donald Ross, 20 April 1847, ibid.; Ross to Mason, 24 April 1847, ibid.

84. William Barnley to the Secretaries of the Wesleyan Missionary Society, 3 February 1846/47?, WMMS Box 104, 1846/48, 14G.

85. Jacobs to the Secretaries of the Wesleyan Missionary Society, 25 July 1848, WMMS Box 104, 1846/48, 14G; 10 December 1849, WMMS Box 105, 1849/51, 15G.

86. Wood to Elijah Hoole, 20 December 1860, Box 108, 1858/63, 18C(1).

87. George Simpson to Enoch Wood, 12 April 1852, WMMS Box 106, 1852/54, 16C; Wood to the Secretaries of the Wesleyan Missionary Society, 29 December 1853, WMMS Box 106, 1852/54, 16C.

88. The Church of England made several attempts to have WMMS missions transferred to its jurisdiction; see, for example, Bishop Anderson to the Secretaries of the Wesleyan Missionary Society, 14 October 1853, WMMS Box 106, 1852/54, 16G; Wood to Bishop Anderson, 2 June 1854, WMMS Box 106, 1852/54, 16C.

89. Woolsey to Elijah Hoole, 1 January 1863, WMMS Box 108, 1858/63, 18C(2).

90. Findlay and Holdsworth, *History* 1:471–75.

CHAPTER 4

1. Chaney, *Birth of Missions*, 75.

2. Daniel Haskell, Preface to *Sixteen Years in the Indian Country: The Journal of Daniel Williams Harmon, 1800–1816*, ed. W. Kaye Lamb (Toronto: Macmillan, 1957), 4.

3. Ibid., 6–7.

4. H. R. Schoolcraft, *Schoolcraft's Expedition to Lake Itasca: The Discovery of the Source of the Mississippi*, ed. Philip P. Mason (East Lansing: Michigan State University Press, 1958), 135–36.

5. Ibid., 43.

6. David Zeisberger, "David Zeisberger's Official Diary, Fairfield, 1791–1795," ed. and trans. Paul Eugene Mueller. *Transactions of the Moravian Historical Society* 19, pt. 1 (1963): 7.

7. Henry A. Jacobson, "Narrative of an Attempt to Establish a Mission Among the Chippewa Indians of Canada, Between the Years 1800 and 1806," *Transactions of the Moravian Historical Society* 5, pt. 1 (1895): 1–24.

8. Zeisberger, "Official Diary," 21–24, 109, 122, 123, 125, 133.

9. Ibid., 135.

10. Ibid., 159.

11. Ibid., 218.

12. Jacobson, "Narrative," 20.

13. Ibid., 22.

14. William Montague Ferry and Amanda White Ferry, "Frontier Mackinac Island, 1823–1834: Letters of William Montague and

Amanda White Ferry," ed. Charles A. Anderson, *Journal of the Presbyterian Historical Society* 26 (1948): 110.

15. Ibid., 114–15.

16. Ibid., 117.

17. Peter Dougherty, "Diaries of Peter Dougherty," ed. Charles A. Anderson, *Journal of the Presbyterian Historical Society* 30 (1952): 104–5.

18. Ibid., 105–6.

19. For further information on Boutwell's career, see Harold C. Hickerson, "William T. Boutwell of the American Board and the Pillager Chippewa: The History of a Failure," *Ethnohistory* 12, no. 1 (1965): 1–29.

20. William Thurston Boutwell, "Diary Kept by the Reverend William Thurston Boutwell, Missionary to the Ojibwa Indians, 1832–1837," William T. Boutwell Papers, Minnesota Historical Society, St. Paul, 23, 24 September 1832; 12 May, 5, 10 October 1833.

21. Ibid., 30 September 1832, 9 June 1834; Sherman Hall to Lydia Hall, 25 December 1832, SH.

22. Boutwell, "Diary," 3, 10 September 1832.

23. Ibid., 27 June 1832.

24. Ibid., 28 June 1832.

25. Ibid., 9 October 1833.

26. Ibid., 1 January 1834.

27. Ibid., 6 January 1834.

28. Ibid., 11 November 1833.

29. Sr. M. Inez Hilger, *Chippewa Child Life and Its Cultural Background*, Smithsonian Institution, Bureau of American Ethnology, Bulletin no. 146 (Washington, D.C.: Government Printing Office, 1951), 39–50.

30. Ibid., 50–55.

31. Boutwell, "Diary," 27 August 1833.

32. Ibid., 7 November 1833.

33. Ibid., 30 January 1833.

34. Ibid., 9 March 1836.

35. Ibid., 18, 26 October; 9 November 1833.

36. Ibid., 28 March 1834. For a description of the sugar camp, see Densmore, *Chippewa Customs*, 122–23.

37. Boutwell, "Diary," 29 March 1834.

38. Ibid., 1 April 1834.

39. Quoted in ibid., 18 October 1836.

40. Ibid., 14 August 1837.

41. William Boutwell to Prudential Committee of the American Board of Commissioners for Foreign Missions, 5 May 1846, Pokegama, Papers of the ABCFM, Missions to the North American Indians,

Houghton Library, Harvard University, Cambridge, Mass. (hereafter cited as ABC), 18.4.1, vol. 1, 41.

42. Edmund F. Ely, Writing book, Ely Family Papers, Minnesota Historical Society, 22, 24, 27 August 1833; see also Densmore, *Chippewa Customs*, 9.

43. Ely, Writing book, 20, 21, 23, 24 September 1833.

44. Ibid., 21, 29 September; 20 October; 7 December; 8 December 1833; 5 January 1834.

45. Ibid., 30 September; 5, 13, 14 October 1833.

46. Ibid., 7 December 1833, 4 May 1834.

47. Ibid., 8 June 1834.

48. Ibid., 2 October 1834.

49. Ibid., 28 October 1834.

50. Ibid., 31 October; 1, 2, 12, 16 November 1834.

51. Ibid., 23 February 1835.

52. Ibid., 1 January 1835.

53. Hilger, *Chippewa Child Life*, 58–59.

54. Ely, Writing book, 23, 31 May; 14 June 1835.

55. Ibid., 30 June; 30 August; 14 September 1835.

56. Ibid., 21 September 1835.

57. Ibid., 19 October 1835.

58. Ibid., 2, 3 November 1835.

59. Ibid., 26, 27 December 1835.

60. Ibid., 13, 14 February; 17 August 1836.

61. Ibid., 22 August, 4 December 1836.

62. Ibid., 27 February 1840, [July/August?] 1842.

63. Ibid., 16 April 1836.

64. Ibid., 20, 21 May; 19 August 1836.

65. Ibid., 6 June 1838.

66. Ibid., 7 August 1838.

67. Quoted in John Adams Vinton et al., "Missionaries of the ABCFM, 1810–1885," 2 vols., Houghton Library, Harvard University, Cambridge, Mass., 1:393–95.

68. Ferry and Ferry, "Frontier Mackinac Island," 103.

69. Albert Keiser, *Lutheran Mission Work Among the American Indians* (Minneapolis: Augsburg, 1922), 60, 64–67, 68 (quote), 73–74.

CHAPTER 5

1. Ritzenthaler, "Southwestern Chippewa"; Edward S. Rogers, "Southeastern Chippewa," in Trigger, *Northeast*, 760–71; Nancy Oestreich Lurie, *Wisconsin Indians* (Madison: State Historical Society of Wisconsin, 1982), 10, 20.

2. Hall to Mr. and Mrs. Aaron Hall, 1 September 1845, SH.

3. Wheeler to Selah B. Treat, 21 July 1852, ABC, 18.4.1, vol. 1, 265.

4. Vinton et al., "Missionaries of the ABCFM," 1:391–95.

5. Hall to Aaron Hall, 9 January 1832, SH; Hall and William Boutwell to David Green, Prudential Committee of the American Board of Commissioners for Foreign Missions, 11 May 1833, ABC 18.2.7, vol. 1, 74–77.

6. Hall to Aaron Hall, 15 June 1832; Hall to Lydia Hall, 25 December 1832, SH.

7. Quote from Hall to Lydia Hall, 15 June 1833; Hall to Aaron Hall, 22 June, 28 August 1833, SH; Hall journal, n.d. [October 1833?].

8. Hall to Laura Hall, 4 February 1835, SH.

9. Hall to Laura Hall Mudget, 11 June 1839; Hall to Aaron Hall, 2 February 1842, SH.

10. P. Chrysostomus Verwyst, O.F.M., *Life and Labors of Rt. Rev. Frederic Baraga, First Bishop of Marquette, Mich., to Which Are Added Short Sketches of the Lives and Labors of Other Indian Missionaries of the Northwest* (Milwaukee: M. H. Wiltzius, 1900), 174–200.

11. Vecsey, *Traditional Ojibwa Religion*, 17.

12. Hall to David Green, 2 September 1844, ABC 18.4.1, vol. 1, 56; Lyle M. Stone and Donald Chaput, "History of the Upper Great Lakes Area," in Trigger, *Northeast*, 602–9; Hall to Lydia [Hall] Burbank, 5 May 1843, SH.

13. Leonard H. Wheeler to David Green, 3 May 1843, ABC 18.3.7, vol. 2, 223.

14. Ibid.

15. Wheeler to Green, 22 March 1843, ABC 18.3.7, vol. 2, 220; Hall to Lydia Burbank, 5 May 1843, SH.

16. Hall to Charles Mudget, n.d. [1846?]; Hall to Lydia Burbank, 30 November 1847, SH; Hall to David Green, 26 January 1846, 10 February 1847, ABC 18.4.1, vol. 1, 60, 66; Vecsey, *Traditional Ojibwa Religion*, 154.

17. Hall to Laura Mudget, 21 March 1851, SH.

18. Wheeler to Green, 5 September 1844, 30 June 1845, ABC 18.4.1, vol. 1, 199, 210; Hall to Green, 18 March 1846, ibid., 62; Wheeler to Selah B. Treat, 29 December 1847, ibid., 205.

19. Harriet Hall to Laura Mudget, 12 March 1850; Hall to Lydia Burbank, 14 January 1851, SH; Wheeler to Treat, 9 July 1851, ABC 18.4.1, vol. 1, 220.

20. Wheeler to Treat, 5 March, 14 July (quote) 1852, ABC 18.4.1, vol. 1, 223, 229.

21. Hall, Annual Mission Report, 1850, ABC 18.4.1, vol. 1, F1; Wheeler to Treat, 3 March 1853, ibid., 231; School Report, La Pointe, 30 June 1852, ibid., 5; Hall to Aaron Hall, 27 October 1852; Hall to Sister [?], 8 May 1853; Harriet Hall to Laura Mudget, 28 February 1855, SH.

22. The Lac Court Oreilles and Red Cliff bands were from Wisconsin; the Keweenaw and Ontonagan bands from Michigan; and the Fond du Lac and Grand Portage bands from Minnesota. See Vecsey, *Traditional Ojibwa Religion,* 17–18. Henry C. Gilbert to George W. Manypenny, 24 April 1855, ABC 18.4.1, vol. 1, 13.

23. Wheeler to Treat, 31 July 1854, 3 January 1855, ibid., 237, 248.

24. Wheeler to Treat, 21 July 1857, ibid., 265. For conversions, see Wheeler to Treat, 19 March, 7 July 1855, ibid., 243, 248; Wheeler to R. Anderson, 17 February 1857, ibid., 264; Wheeler to Treat, 17 March 1861, ABC 18.4.1, vol. 2, 59.

25. Wheeler [to Treat], 3 January 1855, ABC 18.4.1, vol. 1, 248; Wheeler, First report of manual labor boarding school, 11 January 1860, ABC 18.3.1, vol. 2, 14; Wheeler to Treat, 11 August 1860, ibid., 6; Rhoda W. Spicer to Treat, 26 January 1861, ABC 18.4.1, vol. 2, 46.

26. A. P. Truesdell, quoted in S. G. Clark to S. L. Pomroy, 11 May 1858, ABC 18.4.1, vol. 1, 19. David B. Spencer to Treat, 14 August 1862, ABC 18.4.1, vol. 2, 17; Edwin Ells to W. P. Dole, Commissioner of Indian Affairs, 18 January 1864, ibid., 21.

27. Wheeler to Treat, Annual Report, 15 August 1864, ABC 18.4.1, vol. 2, 9; Wheeler to Treat, 21 July 1857, ABC 18.4.2, vol. 1, 265.

28. Wheeler to Treat, 23 August 1861, ABC 18.4.1, vol. 2, 60.

29. Gary C. Anderson, "War (The Little Crow War of 1862 in Minnesota)," in Fixico, *Anthology of Western Great Lakes Indian History,* 353–406; Wheeler to William P. Dole, Commissioner of Indian Affairs, 27 January 1862, ABC 18.4.1, vol. 2, 63.

30. Wheeler [to Treat?], Annual Report, 1 August 1865, ABC 18.4.1, vol. 2, 10; Wheeler to Treat, Annual Report, 12 August 1863, ibid., 8.

31. Blatchford to Treat, 27 August 1868, ABC 18.4.1, vol. 2, 42; Wheeler [in Beloit] to Treat, 10 October 1868, ibid., 104; Blatchford to Treat, 16 August 1869, ibid., [no number]; Wheeler [to Treat?], Annual Report, 1 August 1865, Annual Report, ibid., 10; Wheeler to Treat, 6 March 1866, ibid., 91.

32. Edwin Ells to Treat, 10 November 1868, ABC 18.4.1, vol. 2, 22; Wheeler to Treat, 24 December 1869, 4 July 1870, ibid., 113.

33. Michael C. Coleman, *Presbyterian Missionary Attitudes Toward American Indians, 1837–1893* (Jackson: University Press of Mississippi, 1985), 11–12; Gaius Jackson Slosser, "Walter Lowrie, Mission Organizer," *Journal of the Presbyterian Historical Society* 36 (1958): 3–18; Berkhofer, *Salvation and the Savage*, 172; Harold S. Faust, "The Growth of Presbyterian Missions to the American Indians During the National Period," *Journal of the Presbyterian Historical Society* 22 (1944): 82–123, 137–71.

34. Baird to Lowrie, 22 October 1880, in *American Indian Correspondence: The Presbyterian Historical Society Collection of Missionaries' Letters, 1833–1893* (Westport, Conn.: Greenwood Press, 1979) (hereafter cited as *AIC*), D:1:320. The following letters list converts and inquirers: [?] to Lowrie, 8 March 1884, *AIC* G:1:281; Wright to Ellinwood, 31 October 1885, *AIC* 2:2:104; Baird to Lowrie, 13 May 1878, *AIC* E:1:4; Baird to Lowrie, 27 September 1883, *AIC* G:1:170; Spees to Lowrie, 16 September 1884, *AIC* H:1:74; S. G. Wright to Lowrie, 24 September 1884, *AIC* H:1:77; Wright to Lowrie, 15 January 1885, *AIC* H:1:149; Spees, "Indian Mission Church Report," 5 October 1884, *AIC* H:1:226; Susie Dougherty to Lowrie, 2 January 1885, *AIC* H:1:145.

35. Keiser, *Lutheran Mission Work*, 60, 64–69, 73–74.

36. Wheeler to Treat, 31 July 1858, ABC 18.4.1, vol. 1, 273; Wheeler to Treat, 13 August 1862, ABC 18.4.1, vol. 2, 7.

37. Baird to John C. Lowrie, 14 July 1883, *AIC* G:1:111.

38. Baird to Lowrie, 30 December 1876, *AIC* C:287.

39. Baird to D. C. Mahan, U.S. Indian Agent, 30 March 1878, *AIC* E:1:33.

40. Francis Spees, Monthly Reports, Odanah, 30 May, 30 June, 31 July, 30 September 1884, *AIC* H:1:122, 126, 125, 123; [Susie Dougherty?], Mission Report, Round Lake, [1885?], *AIC* 2:2:309.

41. Minnie Ells to Ellinwood, 20 August 1886, *AIC* 2:2:153; Susie Dougherty to Lowrie, 1 October 1884, *AIC* H:1:82; Spees to Lowrie, 19 November 1884, *AIC* H:1:90.

42. Baird to J. C. Lowrie, 9 December 1880, *AIC* 9:1:342; William H. Leed, Acting Commissioner, Office of Indian Affairs, to Baird, 15 April 1878, *AIC* D:1:126.

43. Baird to Lowrie, 7 February 1883, *AIC* G:1:24.

44. Baird to Lowrie, 24 October 1883, 4 March 1884, *AIC* G:1:192, 279.

45. Spees to Ellinwood, 13 November 1885, *AIC* 2:2:107; Minnie Ells to Ellinwood, 30 November 1885, *AIC* 2:2:110; Edwin Ells to

Ellinwood, 10 December 1885, *AIC* 2:2:113; Blatchford to Ellinwood, 20 August 1886, *AIC* 2:2:155 (quote).

46. Coleman, *Presbyterian Missionary Attitudes*, 14–15.

47. Johanna E. Feest and Christina F. Feest, "Ottawa," in Trigger, *Handbook*, 772–86.

48. Faust, "Growth of Presbyterian Missions," 159.

49. Dougherty to Wells, 28 February 1839, *AIC* 7:3:22. For a group biography of Old School missionaries, see Coleman, *Presbyterian Missionary Attitudes*, 21–22.

50. Ruth Craker, *First Protestant Mission in the Grand Traverse Region*, 2d ed. (Leland, Mich.: Leland Enterprise, 1935), 37, 45.

51. Dougherty to Lowrie, [1838?], *AIC* 7:3:9.

52. Dougherty to Daniel Wells, 18 February 1839, *AIC* 7:3:22.

53. Dougherty to Wells, July 1839, *AIC* 7:3:30.

54. Dougherty to Wells, 19 April 1842, *AIC* 7:3:70; Dougherty to Walter Lowrie, 27 April 1842, 6 July 1843, *AIC* 7:3:71, 96.

55. See, for example, Turner to Walter Lowrie, 29 July 1856, *AIC* 7:1:208; Guthrie to Walter Lowrie, 20 July 1857, *AIC* 7:2:12; Baird to J. C. Lowrie, 24 February, 27 September 1883; 8 March 1884; *AIC* G:1:35, 170, 281; Baird to J. C. Lowrie, 20 May 1880, *AIC* D:1:234.

56. Dougherty to Walter Lowrie, n.d. [1859], *AIC* 7:2:82 1/2.

57. Dougherty to Walter Lowrie, 16 February 1859, *AIC* 7:2:83.

58. Dougherty to Walter Lowrie, 15 April 1859, *AIC* 7:2:89. Methodists established a mission in an Ottawa community at L'Anse in 1842–43 and actively tried to recruit new members from among those the BFM worked with; see Rev. Antoine Ivan Rezek, *History of the Diocese of Sault Ste. Marie and Marquette . . .* , 2 vols. (Houghton, Mich.: N.p., 1907), 2:239. The following letters discuss the problem of Methodist competition: Porter to Lowrie, 26 June, 2 July 1861, *AIC* 7:4:96, 98; Dougherty to Lowrie, 21 March 1862, *AIC* 7:4:121.

59. Dougherty to Mr. McKean, 25 September 1850, *AIC* 7:1:13.

60. Kate McBeth, *The Nez Perce Since Lewis and Clark* (New York: Revell, 1908), 54–55, cited in Coleman, *Presbyterian Missionary Attitudes*, 105.

61. Porter to Walter Lowrie, 12 December 1860, *AIC* 7:4:76.

62. Dougherty to Walter Lowrie, 12 January 1858, 4 January 1859, *AIC* 7:2:49, 80; Porter to Lowrie, 28 May 1861, *AIC* 7:4:93; Baird to John C. Lowrie, 5 July 1877, *AIC* C:336.

63. Dougherty to Wells, July 1839, *AIC* 7:3:30.

64. Dougherty to Schoolcraft, 4 September [1840], *AIC* 7:3:45; Dougherty to Wells, [1841], *AIC* 7:3:54; Maahkewenah et al. to Presbyterian Board of Missions, 26 October 1851, *AIC* 7:1:21; Indians of

Cross Village to the Presbyterian Board of Missions, [1853], *AIC* 7:1:85.

65. Dougherty to Daniel Wells, 11 October 1848, *AIC* 7:3:161.

66. Dougherty to Mr. McKean, 25 September 1850, *AIC* 7:1:13. The following discuss enrollment by gender: Dougherty to Walter Lowrie, 25 December 1848, 1 May 1849, *AIC* 7:3:163, 166; Dougherty to Lowrie, 4 September 1850, *AIC* 7:1:7; Dougherty to P. Babcock, Superintendent of Indian Affairs, Grand Traverse, 14 October 1850, *AIC* 7:1:8.

67. Dougherty to Walter Lowrie, 26 September 1853, *AIC* 7:1:91.

68. Dougherty to Lowrie, 16 January 1854, *AIC* 7:1:108.

69. Dougherty to Lowrie, 8, 22 December 1860; 6 December 1861 (quote); *AIC* 7:4:75, 78, 109. Attendance rosters were submitted irregularly; the following are representative: Annual Report [1844?], *AIC* 7:3:111—49 boys/23 girls; Dougherty to William A. Richmond, Acting Superintendent of Indian Affairs [1846?], *AIC* 7:3:136—44 boys/14 girls; Dougherty to P. Babcock, Superintendent of Indian Affairs, Grand Traverse, 14 October 1850, *AIC* 7:1:8—20 boys/10 girls; Porter, School Report, 12 October 1854, *AIC* 7:1:19—30 boys/14 girls; Dougherty to Lowrie, 14 June 1861, *AIC* 7:4:95—15 boys/8 girls; Dougherty to Lowrie, 20 June 1861, *AIC* 7:4:125—16 boys/7 girls; Dougherty to Lowrie, 17 November 1862, *AIC* 7:4:139—14 boys/11 girls.

70. Porter to Lowrie, 24 March 1853, *AIC* 7:1:59.

71. Dougherty to Lowrie, 5 February 1853, *AIC* 7:1:55; Turner to Lowrie, 30 December 1853, 2 July 1856, *AIC* 7:1:106, 201; Turner to Lowrie, 10 September 1857, *AIC* 7:2:30.

72. Guthrie to Lowrie, 1 January 1857, *AIC* 7:2:2.

73. Turner to Lowrie, 10 September 1857, *AIC* 7:2:30.

74. Turner to Lowrie, 20 September 1857, *AIC* 7:2:45; Guthrie to Lowrie, 22 September 1857, *AIC* 7:2:33.

75. Gosegwad, Speaker [for Middle Village band?]/Robert Daily, interpreter to Executive Committee of Board of Foreign Missions of the Presbyterian Church, 5 January 1858, *AIC* 7:2:48.

76. Turner to Lowrie, 5 January 1858, *AIC* 7:2:47.

77. Rezek, *History*, 234–41; Verwyst, *Life and Labors*, 209–14.

78. Guthrie to Walter Lowrie, 18 January 1856, *AIC* 7:1:185. Guthrie was writing to Lowrie from the Western Theological Seminary in Allegheny, Pennsylvania, following his visit to Little Traverse prior to moving to the station.

79. Porter to Walter Lowrie, October 1853, *AIC* 7:1:99. Although Peter Dougherty apparently had arrived at some understanding

with the local priest, he too feared the pervasive influence of "the papists."

80. Francis Spees to F. F. Ellinwood, 28 June 1885, *AIC* 2:2:78.

81. Berkhofer, *Salvation and the Savage*, 59, 92–95; Coleman, *Presbyterian Missionary Attitudes*, 120.

82. See Coleman, *Presbyterian Missionary Attitudes*, chap. 2, for a discussion of missionaries' expectations of the reception that Indians would give the missions.

83. Dougherty to Walter Lowrie, 22 March 1861, *AIC* 7:4:87; Dougherty, Report of School at Pine Grove [Omena], 6 February 1861, *AIC* 7:4:84; Dougherty to Lowrie, 11 August 1865, 9 January, 4 August 1866, *AIC* B:1:13, 15, 18.

84. Dougherty to J. C. Lowrie, 18 February 1870, *AIC* B:2:14; Craker, *First Protestant Mission*, p. 45.

85. Susie A. Dougherty to Ellinwood, 18 August 1885, *AIC* 2:2:86; Sela Wright to Ellinwood, 26 August 1885, *AIC* 2:2:88. The Dougherty sisters were supported by a $300 per annum stipend each from the Woman Synod Society of Wisconsin, Woman's Board of the Northwest; see Mission Report, Round Lake [1885], *AIC* 2:2:309.

86. Mission Report, Round Lake [1885], *AIC* 2:2:309; S. G. Wright to F. F. Ellinwood, 26 August 1885, *AIC* 2:2:88.

87. Anthony Maria Gachet, "Five Years in America (Cinq Ans en Amérique): Journal of a Missionary Among the Redskins, 1859," trans. Joseph Schafer, *Wisconsin Magazine of History* 18 (1934–35): 201, 195.

88. Ibid., 351–52.

89. John C. Lowrie, *A Manual of the Foreign Missions of the Presbyterian Church in the United States of America* (New York: William Rankin, Jr., 1868), 7.

90. Baird to J. C. Lowrie, 2 March 1877, *AIC* C:310; Baird to Lowrie, 25 August 1883, *AIC* G:1:159 (quote).

91. Porter to Lowrie, 31 October 1847, *AIC* 7:3:150. Coleman (*Presbyterian Missionary Attitudes*, 16) has called the Presbyterians' missionary efforts an "awesomely ambitious cultural destruction and regeneration." He argues, however, that despite certain personal and social motivations, their approach was not a racist one and their goal was to save Indians rather than eliminate them. Berkhofer (*Salvation and the Savage*, 10–15) is less generous in his assessment of missionary attitudes.

92. Baird to John C. Lowrie, 30 December 1876, *AIC* C:287.

93. Baird to John C. Lowrie, 22 October, 9 December 1880, *AIC* D:1:320, 341.

94. Dougherty to Walter Lowrie, 7 March 1854, *AIC* 7:1:114.

95. Leonard Wheeler to David Greene, 23 January 1843, ABC 18.3.7, vol. 2, 219.

96. Wheeler to Treat, 21 July 1857, ABC 18.4.1, vol. 1, 265.

97. "Indian School Papers," *Foreign Missionary* 18 (1859): 122–24, cited in Berkhofer, *Salvation and the Savage*, 42.

98. Diane Barthel's study of native girls in French mission schools in Africa indicates that the students took themselves very seriously as role models of Western culture; see "Women's Educational Experience Under Colonialism: Toward a Diachronic Model," *Signs: Journal of Women in Culture and Society* 11, no. 1 (1985): 137–54.

99. Baird to Dr. I. L. Mahan, 18 August 1876, *AIC* C:253.

100. Spees to F. F. Ellinwood, 16 February 1886, *AIC* 2:2:130.

101. Hilger, *Chippewa Child Life*, 55–58; Ruth Landes, *Ojibwa Woman*, passim.

102. Bear River Quarterly School Reports: 31 March 1860—19 boys/17 girls; 30 June 1860—23 boys; 30 September 1861—23 boys/17 girls; 31 December 1861—20 boys/5 girls; 30 June 1863—17 boys/7 girls; [?] 1864—15 boys/6 girls; 2d quarter 1864—21 boys/9 girls; 3d quarter 1864—11 boys/5 girls; 31 December 1864—15 boys/7 girls (*AIC* 7:4:48, 56, 65–66, 112, 156, 188, 193 [two entries], 199).

103. Peter Dougherty to Walter Lowrie, 15 October 1856, *AIC* 7:1:216; Porter to Walter Lowrie, 3 January 1860, *AIC* 7:4:35.

CHAPTER 6

1. Walter Rauschenbush, "Conceptions of Missions," in *The Social Gospel in America, 1880–1920*, ed. Robert T. Handy (New York: Oxford University Press, 1966), 268–73; Gregory H. Singleton, "Protestant Voluntary Organizations and the Shaping of Victorian America," *American Quarterly* 27, no. 2 (1975): 549–60; Joan Jacobs Brumberg, "Zenanas and Girlless Villages: The Ethnology of American Evangelical Women, 1870–1910," *Journal of American History* 69, no. 2 (1982): 347–71; Andrew T. Roy, "Overseas Mission Policies—An Historical Overview," *Journal of Presbyterian History* 57, no. 3 (1979): 186–228.

2. Hallowell made extensive use of Rorschach tests, as did others who based their studies on his methods and findings; see Hallowell, *Culture and Experience*, 149; Victor Barnouw, *Acculturation and Personality Among the Wisconsin Chippewa*, American Anthropological Association Memoir no. 72 (Menasha, Wis.: American Anthropological Association, 1950); Spindler, *Menomini Women*; Louise Spindler and

George Spindler, "Male and Female Adaptations in Culture Change," *American Anthropologist* 60 (1958): 217–33.

3. Landes, *Ojibwa Woman*, 13 and passim.

4. Robert F. Berkhofer, Jr., *The White Man's Indian: Images of the American Indian from Columbus to the Present* (New York: Vintage Books, 1979), 51–55; George W. Stocking, Jr., *Race, Culture, and Evolution: Essays in the History of Anthropology* (New York: Free Press, 1968), 123, 219–28.

5. Berkhofer, *White Man's Indian*, 62–64; Nancy Oestreich Lurie, "Two Dollars," in *Crossing Cultural Boundaries: The Anthropological Experience*, ed. Solon T. Kimball and James B. Watson (San Francisco: Chandler, 1972), 151–63; Jacob Gruber, "Ethnographic Salvage and the Shaping of Anthropology," *American Anthropologist* 62 (1970): 1289–99; Leacock, "Montagnais-Naskapi Band."

6. See Jennifer S. H. Brown, "A. I. Hallowell and William Berens Revisited," in Cowan, *Papers of the Eighteenth Algonquian Conference*, 17–27, for a discussion of Hallowell's perspective on his Berens River field research, particularly regarding psychological and acculturative models. See also Hallowell, *Culture and Experience*, 127, 287–88, 323.

7. Landes, *Ojibwa Religion*, 3.

8. Hallowell, *Culture and Experience*, 295.

9. Ibid.; Landes, *Ojibwa Religion*, 77; Landes, *Ojibwa Woman*, v, 5–6, and passim.

10. Hallowell, *Culture and Experience*, 150; A. Tanner, *Bringing Home Animals*.

11. Hallowell, *Culture and Experience*, 305.

12. Ruth Landes, *Ojibwa Woman*, 10; Hallowell, *Culture and Experience*, 305, 360–62.

13. Landes, *Ojibwa Woman*, v.

14. Landes, *Ojibwa Woman*, 177.

15. See Eric Hobsbawm, "Introduction: Inventing Traditions," in *The Invention of Tradition*, ed. Eric Hobsbawm and Terence Ranger (Cambridge: Cambridge University Press, 1983), 1–14.

16. Landes, *Ojibwa Woman*, 11.

17. Spindler, *Menomini Women*, 16.

18. Landes, *Ojibwa Woman*, 5, 30, 124; Crashing Thunder, *Crashing Thunder: The Autobiography of an American Indian*, ed. Paul Radin (New York: D. Appleton, 1926), 60; Mountain Wolf Woman, *Mountain Wolf Woman, Sister of Crashing Thunder: The Autobiography of a Winnebago Indian*, ed. Nancy Oestreich Lurie (Ann Arbor: University of Michigan Press, 1961), 22.

19. Landes, *Ojibwa Religion*, 12. Hallowell, *Culture and Experience*, 295–97, 299. Adrian Tanner (*Bringing Home Animals*, 137–38) has noted similar terminology used in Cree hunting bands.

20. See Leacock, "Women's Status in Egalitarian Society," 247–75, for a discussion of the contradictions between Landes's description and her analysis, through what Leacock calls "the downgrading of women that is built into unexamined and ethnocentric phraseology." On gender biases in anthropological studies, see also Rayna Green, *Native American Women: A Contextual Bibliography* (Bloomington: Indiana University Press, 1983), intro.; Ruby Rohrlich-Leavitt, Barbara Sykes, and Elizabeth Weatherford, "Aboriginal Woman: Male and Female Anthropological Perspectives," in *Toward an Anthropology of Women*, ed. Rayna R. Reiter (New York: Monthly Review Press, 1975), 110–26; and Sharon W. Tiffany, "Introduction: Theoretical Issues in the Anthropological Study of Women," in *Women and Society: An Anthropological Reader*, ed. Sharon W. Tiffany (St. Albans, Vt.: Eden Press Women's Publications, 1979), 1–35.

21. Methodists had first visited Berens River during James Evans's stay at Norway House in the 1840s and later established a permanent mission in 1893; see Vecsey, *Traditional Ojibwa Religion*, 32.

22. Speck, *Naskapi*, 77, 95, 102, 109–10, 115, 231.

23. Leacock, "Montagnais Women."

24. Jenness, *Ojibwa Indians of Parry Island*, 97, also 51; Densmore, *Chippewa Customs*; Hilger, *Chippewa Child Life*, 54–55.

25. Jenness, *Ojibwa Indians of Parry Island*, 97.

26. Ibid., 60, 97, 100; Speck, *Naskapi*, 175, 231.

27. A. Tanner, *Bringing Home Animals*, 76–79, 119, 125, 130, 180, 211.

28. Leacock, "Women's Status in Egalitarian Society." As Leacock has pointed out, it is a fallacy to presume that hunter-gatherer societies consisted of nuclear families in which women were bound to individual men.

29. Thomas G. Harding, "Adaptation and Stability," in *Evolution and Culture*, ed. Marshall D. Sahlins and Elman R. Service (Ann Arbor: University of Michigan Press, 1960), 45–68.

30. Felicia Ifeoma Ekejiuba, "Introduction to Women and Symbolic Systems," *Signs: Journal of Women in Culture and Society* 3 (1977): 90–92.

31. Axtell, *Invasion Within*; and Vecsey, *Traditional Ojibwa Religion*.

32. Eleanor Burke Leacock, Introduction to *North American Indians in Historical Perspective*, ed. Eleanor Burke Leacock and Nancy Oestreich Lurie (New York: Random House, 1971), 3–28.

33. Van Kirk, *"Many Tender Ties"*; Jennifer S. H. Brown, *Strangers in Blood: Fur Trade Company Families in Indian Country* (Vancouver: University of British Columbia Press, 1980).

34. Van Kirk, *"Many Tender Ties,"* 17.

35. Ibid., 6–7, 16, 17. Van Kirk assumes that women's status in native society was secondary and that women were the possessions of men; she refers to Indians and "their women" (24). See also Wright, "Economic Development and Native American Women," for a similar argument using the example of Coastal Salish women.

36. Robin Fisher, review of *"Many Tender Ties,"* by Sylvia Van Kirk, *Canadian Historical Review* 64, no. 2 (1983): 237–38.

37. Perry, "Fur Trade and the Status of Women."

38. Coleman, *Presbyterian Missionary Attitudes*, 94–95, 127; Charlotte J. Frisbie, "Traditional Navajo Women: Ethnographic and Life History Portrayals," *American Indian Quarterly* 6 (1982): 11–33; Mary Shepardson, "The Status of Navajo Women," *American Indian Quarterly* 6 (1982): 149–69.

39. Landes, *Ojibwa Woman*, 16. Gerald Vizenor, in *The People Named the Chippewa: Narrative Histories* (Minneapolis: University of Minnesota Press, 1984), 3–4, describes Nenebush, or Naanabozho, as "the compassionate woodland trickster, [who] wanders in mythic time and transformational space between tribal experiences and dreams. The trickster is related to plants and animals and trees; he is a teacher and healer in various personalities who, as numerous stories reveal, explains the values of healing plants, wild rice, maple sugar, basswood, and birch bark to woodland tribal people. More than a magnanimous teacher and transformer, the trickster is capable of violence, deceptions, and cruelties: the realities of human imperfections. The woodland trickster is an existential shaman in the comic mode, not an isolated and sentimental tragic hero in conflict with nature. The trickster is comic in the sense that he does not reclaim idealistic ethics, but survives as a part of the natural world; he represents a spiritual balance in a comic drama rather than the romantic elimination of human contradictions and evil."

40. Jeanne Guillemin, *Urban Renegades: The Cultural Strategy of American Indians* (New York: Columbia University Press, 1975), 87, 88, 96, 218.

41. Ibid., 98–99, 100–101 (quote).

42. Spindler, *Menomini Women*, 27, 37, 99.

43. Spindler and Spindler, "Male and Female Adaptations."

44. Hallowell, *Culture and Experience*, 364; Mountain Wolf Woman,

Autobiography, 100–101; Crashing Thunder, *Autobiography*, xx and passim; Henrikson, *Hunters in the Barrens*, 77; Dunning, *Social and Economic Change*, 131.

45. Regina Flannery, "Gossip as a Clue to Attitudes," *Primitive Man* 7 (1934): 8–12.

Selected Bibliography

ARCHIVAL SOURCES

American Board of Commissioners of Foreign Missions. Missions to the North American Indians. Papers. Houghton Library, Harvard University, Cambridge, Mass.

American Indian Correspondence. The Presbyterian Historical Society Collection of Missionaries' Letters, 1833–1893 (microfilm). Westport, Conn.: Greenwood Press, 1979.

Bacon, D. A., ed. "Wesleyan Methodist Church (Great Britain)." 4 vols. United Methodist Archives and History Center, Madison, N.J.

Boutwell, William Thurston. "Diary Kept by the Reverend William Thurston Boutwell, Missionary to the Ojibwa Indians, 1832–1837." William T. Boutwell Papers, Minnesota Historical Society, St. Paul, Minn.

Ely, Edmund F. Writing book. Ely Family Papers, Minnesota Historical Society, St. Paul, Minn.

Hall, Sherman. Papers. Minnesota Historical Society, St. Paul, Minn.

Vinton, John Adams, et al. "Missionaries of the ABCFM, 1810–1885." 2 vols. Houghton Library, Harvard University, Cambridge, Mass.

Wesleyan Methodist Missionary Society Archives. London–North American Correspondence. Microfiche. United Methodist Archives and History Center, Madison, N.J.

PRINTED PRIMARY SOURCES

Boucher, Pierre. *True and Genuine Description of New France, Commonly Called Canada, and of the Manners and Customs and Productions of That Country* (1664). Translated by Edward Louis Montizambert. Montreal: George E. Desbarats, 1883.

Cameron, Duncan. "The Nipigon Country, 1804, with Extracts from His Journal." In *Les bourgeois de la Compagnie du Nord-Ouest: Récits de voyages, lettres et rapports inédits relatifs au Nord-Ouest canadien*, edited by L. R. Masson, 2:229–300. Quebec: A. Cote, 1889–90; reprinted New York: Antiquarian Press, 1960.

Chaboillez, Charles. "Journal of Charles Jean Baptiste Chaboillez, 1797–1798." Edited by Harold Hickerson. *Ethnohistory* 6, no. 3 (1959): 265–316; 6, no. 4 (1959): 363–427.

Coues, Elliot, ed. *New Light on the Early History of the Greater Northwest: The Manuscript Journals of Alexander Henry and of David Thompson*. 2 vols. Minneapolis: Ross & Haines, 1965.

Crashing Thunder. *Crashing Thunder: The Autobiography of an American Indian*. Edited by Paul Radin. New York: D. Appleton, 1926.

Denys, Nicolas. *The Description and Natural History of the Coasts of North America (Acadia)* (1672). Translated and edited by William F. Ganong. Toronto: Champlain Society, 1908; reprinted New York: Greenwood Press, 1968.

Diereville, sieur de. *Relation of the Voyage to Port Royal in Acadia of New France* (1708). Translated by Mrs. Clarence Webster, edited by John Clarence Webster. Toronto: Champlain Society, 1933.

Dixon, James. *Personal Narrative of a Tour Through a Part of the United States and Canada: With Notices of the History and Institutions of Methodism in America*. New York: Lane & Scott, 1849.

Dougherty, Peter. "Diaries of Peter Dougherty." Edited by Charles A. Anderson. *Journal of the Presbyterian Historical Society* 30 (1952): 95–114, 175–92, 236–53.

Evans, James. "Letters of Rev. James Evans, Methodist Missionary, Written During His Journey to and Residence in the Lake Superior Region, 1838–39." Edited by Fred Landon. *Ontario History* 28 (1932): 47–70.

Ferry, William Montague, and Amanda White Ferry. "Frontier Mackinac Island, 1823–1834: Letters of William Montague and Amanda White Ferry." Edited by Charles A. Anderson. *Journal of the Presbyterian Historical Society* 25 (1947): 192–222; 26 (1948): 101–27, 182–91.

Gachet, Anthony Maria. "Five Years in America (Cinq Ans en Amérique): Journal of a Missionary Among the Redskins, 1859." Translated by Joseph Schafer. *Wisconsin Magazine of History* 18 (1934–35): 66–76, 191–204, 345–59.

Grant, Peter. "The Sauteux Indians About 1804." In *Les bourgeois de la Compagnie du Nord-Ouest: Récits de voyages, lettres et rapports inédits relatifs au Nord-Ouest Canadien*, edited by L. R. Masson, 2:303–66. Quebec: A. Cote, 1889–90; reprinted New York: Antiquarian Society, 1960.

Haskell, Daniel. Preface to *Sixteen Years in the Indian Country: The Journal of Daniel Williams Harmon, 1800–1816*. Edited by W. Kaye Lamb. Toronto: Macmillan, 1957.

Isham, James. *James Isham's Observations on Hudsons Bay, 1743; and Notes and Observations on a Book Entitled "A Voyage to Hudsons Bay in* the Dobbs Galley, 1749." Edited by E. E. Rich. Toronto: Champlain Society, 1949.

Jacobs, Peter. *Journal of the Reverend Peter Jacobs, Indian Wesleyan Missionary, from Rice Lake to the Hudson's Bay Territory, and Returning. Commencing May, 1852. With a Brief Account of His Life and a Short History of the Wesleyan Mission in That Country.* New York: Printed by the author, 1857.

Jacobson, Henry A. "Narrative of an Attempt to Establish a Mission Among the Chippewa Indians of Canada, Between the Years 1800 and 1806." *Transactions of the Moravian Historical Society* 5, no. 1 (1895): 1–24.

Keith, George. "Letters to Mr. Roderic McKenzie, 1807–1817." In *Les bourgeois de la Compagnie du Nord-Ouest: Récits de voyages, lettres et rapports inédits relatifs au Nord-Ouest canadien*, edited by L. R. Masson, 2:61–132. Quebec: A. Cote, 1889–90; reprinted New York: Antiquarian Society, 1960.

Kelsey, Henry. *The Kelsey Papers.* Ottawa: Public Archives of Canada and Public Record Office of Northern Ireland, 1929.

Lahontan, Louis Armand de Lom d'Arce, baron de. *New Voyages to North America* (1703). 2 vols. Edited by Reuben Gold Thwaites. New York: Burt Franklin, 1905; reprinted New York: Lenox Hill, 1970.

Le Clercq, Chrestien. *New Relation of Gaspesia: With the Customs and Religion of the Gaspesian Indians* (1691). Translated and edited by William F. Ganong. Toronto: Champlain Society, 1910; reprinted New York: Greenwood Press, 1968.

Lescarbot, Marc. *Nova Francia, a Description of Acadia* (1606). New York: Harper, 1928.

——— . *The History of New France* (1609). Translated by W. L. Grant. 3 vols. Toronto: Champlain Society, 1907–14; reprinted New York: Greenwood Press, 1968.

L'Incarnation, Marie de. *Word from New France: The Selected Letters of Marie de l'Incarnation.* Translated and edited by Joyce Marshall. Toronto: Oxford University Press, 1967.

Long, Stephen H. *Narrative of an Expedition to the Source of St. Peter's River, Lake Winnepeek, Lake of the Woods, &c. Performed in the Years 1823, by Order of the Hon. J. C. Calhoun, Secretary of War, Under the Command of Stephen H. Long, U.S.A.* (1824). Edited by William H. Keating. Minneapolis: Ross & Haines, 1959.

Lowrie, John C. *A Manual of the Foreign Missions of the Presbyterian Church in the United States of America.* New York: William Rankin, Jr., 1868.

McDonnell, John. "Some Account of the Red River (About 1797), with Extracts from His Journal, 1793–1795." In *Les bourgeois de la Compagnie du Nord-Ouest: Récits de voyages, lettres et rapports inédits relatifs au Nord-Ouest canadien*, edited by L. R. Masson, 1:265–95. Quebec: A. Cote, 1889–90; reprinted New York: Antiquarian Press, 1960.

McKenzie, James. "The King's Posts and Journal of a Canoe Jaunt Through the King's Domains, 1808: The Saguenay and the Labrador Coast." In *Les bourgeois de la Compagnie du Nord-Ouest: Récits de voyages, lettres et rapports inédits relatifs au Nord-Ouest canadien*, edited by L. R. Masson, 2:401–54. Quebec: A. Cote, 1889–90; reprinted New York: Antiquarian Press, 1960.

Mountain Wolf Woman. *Mountain Wolf Woman, Sister of Crashing Thunder: The Autobiography of a Winnebago Indian*. Edited by Nancy Oestreich Lurie. Ann Arbor: University of Michigan Press, 1961.

Nelson, George. *"The Orders of the Dreamed": George Nelson on Cree and Northern Ojibwa Religion and Myth*. Edited by Jennifer S. H. Brown and Robert Brightman. Manitoba Studies in History, vol. 3. St. Paul: Minnesota Historical Society, 1988.

Schoolcraft, Henry R. *Schoolcraft's Expedition to Lake Itasca: The Discovery of the Source of the Mississippi*. Edited by Philip P. Mason. East Lansing: Michigan State University Press, 1958.

Tanner, John. *Narrative of the Captivity and Adventures of John Tanner (U.S. Interpreter at the Sault de Ste. Marie) During Thirty Years Residence Among the Indians in the Interior of North America*. Edited by Edwin James. New York: G. & C. & H. Carvil, 1830.

Thompson, David. *David Thompson's Narrative of His Explorations in Western America, 1784–1812*. Edited by J. B. Tyrrell. Toronto: Champlain Society, 1916; reprinted New York: Greenwood Press, 1968.

Thwaites, Reuben Gold, ed. *The Jesuit Relations and Allied Documents: Travels and Explorations of the Jesuit Missionaries in New France, 1610–1791*. 73 vols. Cleveland: Burrows, 1896–1901; reprinted New York: Pageant, 1959.

Turnor, Philip. *Journals of Samuel Hearne and Philip Turnor*. Edited by J. B. Tyrrell. Toronto: Champlain Society, 1934.

Umfreville, Edward. *The Present State of Hudson's Bay, Containing a Full Description of That Settlement and the Adjacent Country and Likewise of the Fur Trade, with Hints for Its Improvement*. London, 1790.

Wentzel, Willard Ferdinand. "Letters to the Hon. Roderic McKenzie, 1807–1824." In *Les bourgeois de la Compagnie du Nord-Ouest: Récits de voyages, lettres et rapports inédits relatifs au Nord-Ouest canadien*, edited by L. R. Masson, 1:67–153. Quebec: A. Cote, 1889–90; reprinted New York: Antiquarian Press, 1960.

West, John. *The Substance of a Journal During a Residence at the Red River Colony*. London: Seeley, 1824; reprinted New York: Johnson Reprint, 1966.

Zeisberger, David. "David Zeisberger's Official Diary, Fairfield, 1791–1795." Edited and translated by Paul Eugene Mueller. *Transactions of the Moravian Historical Society* 19, pt. 1 (1963).

SECONDARY SOURCES

Aaronson, Rande S. "Workers and Wages in the Canadian Fur Trade, 1773–1775." Unpublished paper.

Allen, Paula Gunn. *The Sacred Hoop: Recovering the Feminine in American Indian Traditions*. Boston: Beacon Press, 1986.

Anderson, Gary C. "War (The Little Crow War of 1862 in Minnesota)." In *An Anthology of Western Great Lakes Indian History*, edited by Donald L. Fixico, 353–406. Milwaukee: University of Wisconsin Press, 1987.

Anderson, Karen. "Commodity Exchange and Subordination: Montagnais-Naskapi and Huron Women, 1600–1650." *Signs: Journal of Women in Culture and Society* 11, no. 1 (1985): 49–62.

Axtell, James. *The European and the Indian: Essays in the Ethnohistory of Colonial North America*. New York: Oxford University Press, 1981.

———. *The Invasion Within: The Contest of Cultures in Colonial North America*. New York: Oxford University Press, 1985.

Bailey, Alfred Goldsworthy. *The Conflict of European and Eastern Algonkian Cultures, 1504–1700: A Study in Canadian Civilization*. New Brunswick Museum Monographic Series, no. 2. St. John, 1937; reprinted Toronto: University of Toronto Press, 1979.

Bangert, William V., S.J. *A History of the Society of Jesus*. St. Louis: Institute of Jesuit Sources, 1972.

Barclay, Wade Crawford. *History of Methodist Missions*. Vol. 1: *Early American Methodism, 1769–1844*. New York: Board of Missions and Church Extension of the Methodist Church, 1949–50.

Barnouw, Victor. *Acculturation and Personality Among the Wisconsin Chippewa*. American Anthropological Association Memoir no. 72. Menasha, Wis.: American Anthropological Association, 1950.

Barthel, Diane. "Women's Educational Experience Under Colonialism: Toward a Diachronic Model." *Signs: Journal of Women in Culture and Society* 11, no. 1 (1985): 137–54.

Berkhofer, Robert F., Jr. "The Political Context of a New Indian History." *Pacific Historical Review* 40 (1971): 357–82.

———. *Salvation and the Savage: An Analysis of Protestant Missions and American Indian Response, 1787–1862*. Lexington: University of Kentucky Press, 1965.

———. *The White Man's Indian: Images of the American Indian from Columbus to the Present*. New York: Vintage Books, 1979.

Bishop, Charles A. *The Northern Ojibwa and the Fur Trade: An Historical and Ecological Study*. Montreal: Holt, Rinehart & Winston, 1974.

Bishop, Charles A., and Shepard Krech III. "Matriorganization: The Basis of Aboriginal Subarctic Social Organization." *Arctic Anthropology* 17, no. 2 (1980): 34–45.

Boatman, John. "Historical Overview of the Wisconsin Area: From Early Years to the French, British, and Americans." In *An Anthology of Western Great Lakes Indian History*, edited by Donald L. Fixico, 13–68. Milwaukee: University of Wisconsin Press, 1987.

Bock, Philip K. "Micmac." In *Handbook of North American Indians*, vol. 15: *Northeast*, edited by Bruce G. Trigger, 109–22. Washington, D.C.: Smithsonian Institution, 1978.

Bowden, Henry Warner. *American Indians and Christian Missions: Studies in Conflict*. Chicago: University of Chicago Press, 1981.

Boyer, Paul, and Stephen Nissenbaum. *Salem Possessed: The Social Origins of Witchcraft*. Cambridge, Mass.: Harvard University Press, 1974.

Brown, Jennifer S. H. "A. I. Hallowell and William Berens Revisited." In *Papers of the Eighteenth Algonquian Conference*, edited by William Cowan, 17–27. Ottawa: Carlton University Press, 1987.

———. "The Cure and Feeding of Windigos: A Critique." *American Anthropologist* 73 (1971): 19–22.

———. "Duncan Cameron." In *Dictionary of Canadian Biography*, edited by Francess G. Halpenny, 7:137–39. Toronto: University of Toronto Press, 1988.

———. *Strangers in Blood: Fur Trade Company Families in Indian Country*. Vancouver: University of British Columbia Press, 1980.

Brown, Judith. "Iroquois Women: An Ethnohistoric Note." In *Toward an Anthropology of Women*, edited by Rayna R. Reiter, 235–51. New York: Monthly Review Press, 1975.

Brumberg, Joan Jacobs. "Zenanas and Girlless Villages: The Ethnology of American Evangelical Women, 1870–1910." *Journal of American History* 69, no. 2 (1982): 347–71.

Buffalohead, Priscilla K. "Farmers, Warriors, Traders: A Fresh Look at Ojibway Women." *Minnesota History* 48 (Summer 1983): 236–44.

Campeau, Lucien, S.J. "Roman Catholic Missions in New France." In *Handbook of North American Indians*, vol. 4: *History of Indian-White Relations*, edited by Wilcomb E. Washburn, 464–71. Washington, D.C.: Smithsonian Institution, 1988.

Chaney, Charles L. *The Birth of Missions in America*. South Pasadena, Calif.: William Carey Library, 1976.

Coleman, Michael C. *Presbyterian Missionary Attitudes Toward American Indians, 1837–1893*. Jackson: University Press of Mississippi, 1985.

Cowan, Ruth Schwartz. *More Work for Mother: The Ironies of Household Technology, from the Open Hearth to the Microwave*. New York: Basic Books, 1983.

Craker, Ruth. *First Protestant Mission in the Grand Traverse Region*. 2d ed. Leland, Mich.: Leland Enterprise, 1935.

Dauphin, Cecile, et al. "Women's Culture and Women's Power: An Attempt at Historiography." *Journal of Women's History* 1 (1989): 63–88.

Davies, K. G. "Henry Kelsey." In *Dictionary of Canadian Biography*, edited by Francess G. Halpenny, 2:307–15. Toronto: University of Toronto Press, 1969.

Densmore, Frances. *Chippewa Customs*. Smithsonian Institution, Bureau of American Ethnology, Bulletin no. 86. Washington, D.C.: Government Printing Office, 1929.

Devens, Carol. "Separate Confrontations: Gender as a Factor in Indian Adaptation to European Colonization in New France." *American Quarterly* 38, no. 3 (Bibliography, 1986): 461–80.

Dewdney, Selwyn. *The Sacred Scrolls of The Southern Ojibwa*. Toronto: University of Toronto Press, 1975.

Draper, Patricia. "!Kung Women: Contrasts in Sexual Egalitarianism in Foraging and Sedentary Contexts." In *Toward an Anthropology of Women*, edited by Rayna R. Reiter, 77–109. New York: Monthly Review Press, 1975.

Dunning, R. W. *Social and Economic Change Among the Northern Ojibwa*. Toronto: University of Toronto Press, 1959.

Eccles, W. J. *The Canadian Frontier, 1534–1760*. New York: Holt, Rinehart & Winston, 1969.

Ehrenreich, Barbara, and Deirdre English. *Complaints and Disorders: The Sexual Politics of Sickness*. Old Westbury, N.Y.: Feminist Press, 1973.

Ekejiuba, Felicia Ifeoma. "Introduction to Women and Symbolic Systems." *Signs: Journal of Women in Culture and Society* 3, no. 1 (1977): 90–92.

Epstein, Barbara Leslie. *The Politics of Domesticity: Women, Evangelism, and Temperance in Nineteenth-Century America*. Middletown, Conn.: Wesleyan University Press, 1981.

Etienne, Mona. "Women and Men, Cloth and Colonization: The Transformation of Production-Distribution Relations Among the Baule (Ivory Coast)." In *Women and Colonization: Anthropological Perspectives*, edited by Mona Etienne and Eleanor Leacock, 214–38. New York: Praeger, 1980.

Faust, Harold S. "The Growth of Presbyterian Missions to the American Indians During the National Period." *Journal of the Presbyterian Historical Society* 22 (1944): 82–123, 137–71.

Feest, Johanna E., and Christina F. Feest. "Ottawa." In *Handbook of North American Indians*, vol. 15: *Northeast*, edited by Bruce E. Trigger, 772–86. Washington, D.C.: Smithsonian Institution, 1978.

Findlay, G. G., and W. W. Holdsworth. *The History of the Wesleyan Methodist Missionary Society*. 5 vols. London: Epworth, 1821.

Fisher, Robin. Review of *"Many Tender Ties,"* by Sylvia Van Kirk. *Canadian Historical Review* 64, no. 2 (1983): 234–38.

Flannery, Regina. "Gossip as a Clue to Attitudes." *Primitive Man* 7 (1934): 8–12.

Fogelson, Raymond D. "Psychological Theories of Windigo 'Psychosis' and a Preliminary Application of a Models Approach." In *Context and Meaning in Cultural Anthropology*, edited by Melford E. Spiro, 74–99. New York: Free Press, 1965.

Frisbie, Charlotte J. "Traditional Navajo Women: Ethnographic and Life History Portrayals." *American Indian Quarterly* 6 (1982): 11–33.

Gonzalez, Ellice Becker. "The Changing Economic Roles for Micmac Men and Women: An Ethnohistorical Analysis." Ph.D. diss., State University of New York at Stony Brook, 1979.

Gough, Barry M. "Alexander Henry." In *Dictionary of Canadian Biography*, edited by Francess G. Halpenny, 5:418–19. Toronto: University of Toronto Press, 1983.

Graham, Elizabeth. *Medicine Man to Missionary: Missionaries as Agents of Change Among the Indians of Southern Ontario, 1784–1867*. Toronto: Peter Martin, 1975.

Grant, John Webster. "Missionaries and Messiahs in the Northwest." *Studies in Religion/Sciences religieuses* 9, no. 2 (1980): 125–36.

———. *Moon of Wintertime: Missionaries and the Indians of Canada in Encounter Since 1534*. Toronto: University of Toronto Press, 1984.

Green, Rayna. *Native American Women: A Contextual Bibliography*. Bloomington: Indiana University Press, 1983.

Greven, Philip. *The Protestant Temperament: Patterns of Childrearing, Religious Experience, and the Self in Early America*. New York: Meridian, 1977.

Gruber, Jacob. "Ethnographic Salvage and the Shaping of Anthropology." *American Anthropologist* 62 (1970): 1289–99.

Guillemin, Jeanne. *Urban Renegades: The Cultural Strategy of American Indians*. New York: Columbia University Press, 1975.

Hallowell, A. Irving. *Culture and Experience*. Philadelphia: University of Pennsylvania Press, 1955.

Harding, Thomas G. "Adaptation and Stability." In *Evolution and Culture*, edited by Marshall D. Sahlins and Elman R. Service, 45–68. Ann Arbor: University of Michigan Press, 1960.

Hawkins, Ernest. *Historical Notices of the Missions of the Church of England in the North American Colonies, Previous to the Independence of the United States: Chiefly from the M. S. Documents of the Society for the Propagation of the Gospel in Foreign Parts*. London: B. Fellowes, 1845.

Henriksen, Georg. *Hunters in the Barrens: The Naskapi on the Edge of the White Man's World*. Newfoundland Social and Economic Studies, no. 12. [St. John's,] Newfoundland: Institute of Social and Economic Research, Memorial University of Newfoundland, 1973.

Hickerson, Harold. "The Chippewa of the Upper Great Lakes: A Study in Sociopolitical Change." In *North American Indians in Historical Perspective*, edited by Eleanor Burke Leacock and Nancy Oestreich Lurie, 169–99. New York: Random House, 1971.

——— . "Notes on the Post-Contact Origin of the Midewiwin." *Ethnohistory* 9 (1962): 406–23.

——— . "William T. Boutwell of the American Board and the Pillager Chippewa: The History of a Failure." *Ethnohistory* 12, no. 1 (1965): 1–29.

Hilger, Sr. M. Inez. *Chippewa Child Life and Its Cultural Background*. Smithsonian Institution, Bureau of American Ethnology, Bulletin no. 146. Washington, D.C.: Government Printing Office, 1951.

Hobsbawm, Eric. "Introduction: Inventing Traditions." In *The Invention of Tradition*, edited by Eric Hobsbawm and Terence Ranger, 1–14. Cambridge: Cambridge University Press, 1983.

Horsman, Reginald. "Well-trodden Paths and Fresh Byways: Recent Writing on Native American History." *Reviews in American History* 10, no. 4 (1982): 234–44.

Hutchison, William R. *Errand to the World: American Protestant Thought and Foreign Missions*. Chicago: University of Chicago Press, 1987.

Innis, Harold A. *The Fur Trade in Canada: An Introduction to Canadian Economic History.* Rev. ed. Toronto: University of Toronto Press, 1956.

Jaenen, Cornelius J. "Amerindian Views of French Culture in the Seventeenth Century." *Canadian Historical Review* 55, no. 3 (1974): 261–91.

———. "Conceptual Frameworks for French Views of America and Amerindians." *French Colonial Studies* 2 (1978): 1–22.

———. *Friend and Foe: Aspects of French-Amerindian Cultural Contact in the Sixteenth and Seventeenth Centuries.* New York: Columbia University Press, 1976.

Janes, Robert R., and Jane H. Kelley. "Observations on Crisis Cult Activities in the Mackenzie Basin." In *Problems in the Prehistory of the North American Subarctic: The Athapaskan Question,* edited by J. W. Helmer, S. Van Dyke, and F. J. Kense, 153–64. Calgary: Archaeological Association of the University of Calgary, 1977.

Jenness, Diamond. *The Ojibwa Indians of Parry Island: Their Social and Religious Life.* Canada Department of Mines, National Museum of Canada, Bulletin no. 78, Anthropological Series, no. 17. Ottawa: J. O. Pantenuade, 1935.

Keiser, Albert. *Lutheran Mission Work Among the American Indians.* Minneapolis: Augsburg, 1922.

Kennedy, J. H. *Jesuit and Savage in New France.* New Haven: Yale University Press, 1950.

Kitch, Sally. *Chaste Liberation: Celibacy and Female Cultural Status.* Urbana: University of Illinois Press, 1989.

Landes, Ruth. "The Abnormal Among the Ojibwa Indians." *Journal of Abnormal and Social Psychology* 33 (1938): 14–33.

———. *Ojibwa Religion and the Midewiwin.* Madison: University of Wisconsin Press, 1968.

———. *The Ojibwa Woman.* New York: Norton Library, 1971.

Leacock, Eleanor. Introduction to *North American Indians in Historical Perspective,* edited by Eleanor Burke Leacock and Nancy Oestreich Lurie, 3–28. New York: Random House, 1971.

———. "Matrilocality in a Simple Hunting Economy (Montagnais-Naskapi)." *Southwestern Journal of Anthropology* 11, no. 1 (1955): 31–47.

———. "The Montagnais 'Hunting Territory' and the Fur Trade." *American Anthropological Association Memoirs,* no. 78. Menasha, Wis.: American Anthropological Association, 1954.

———. "The Montagnais-Naskapi Band." In *Contributions to Anthropology: Band Societies,* edited by David Damas, 1–17. National Museum of Canada, Bulletin no. 228, Anthropological Series, no. 84. Ottawa: The Queen's Printer, 1969.

———. "Montagnais Women and the Jesuit Program for Colonization." In *Women and Colonization: Anthropological Perspectives*, edited by Mona Etienne and Eleanor Leacock, 25–42. New York: Praeger, 1980.

———. "Seventeenth-Century Montagnais Social Relations and Values." In *Handbook of North American Indians*, vol. 6: *Subarctic*, edited by June Helm, 190–95. Washington, D.C.: Smithsonian Institution, 1981.

———. "Women's Status in Egalitarian Society: Implications for Social Evolution." *Current Anthropology* 19, no. 2 (1978): 247–75.

Long, John S. "*Manitu*, Power, Books, and *Wiihtikow*: Some Factors in the Adoption of Christianity by Nineteenth-Century Western James Bay Cree." *Native Studies Review* 3, no. 1 (1987): 1–30.

Lougee, Carolyn C. *Le Paradis des Femmes: Women, Salons, and Social Stratification in Seventeenth-Century France*. Princeton: Princeton University Press, 1976.

Lurie, Nancy Oestreich. "Two Dollars." In *Crossing Cultural Boundaries: The Anthropological Experience*, edited by Solon T. Kimball and James B. Watson, 151–63. San Francisco: Chandler, 1972.

———. *Wisconsin Indians*. Madison: State Historical Society of Wisconsin, 1982.

McLean, John. *James Evans: Inventor of the Syllabic System of the Cree Language*. Toronto: Methodist Mission Room, 1890.

McLoughlin, William G., Jr. *Modern Revivalism: Charles Grandison Finney to Billy Graham*. New York: Ronald Press, 1959.

Martin, Calvin. "The Four Lives of a Micmac Copper Pot." *Ethnohistory* 22, no. 2 (1975): 111–33.

———. *Keepers of the Game: Indian-Animal Relationships and the Fur Trade*. Berkeley and Los Angeles: University of California Press, 1978.

———. "Subarctic Indians and Wildlife." In *Old Trails and New Directions: Papers of the Third North American Fur Trade Conference*, edited by Carol M. Judd and Arthur J. Ray, 73–81. Toronto: University of Toronto Press, 1979.

Morgan, Edmund S. *American Slavery, American Freedom: The Ordeal of Colonial Virginia*. New York: Norton, 1975.

Morice, A. G. *History of the Catholic Church in Western Canada, from Lake Superior to the Pacific (1659–1895)*. 2 vols. Toronto: Musson, 1910.

Muir, Elizabeth. "The Bark School House: Methodist Episcopal Missionary Women in Upper Canada, 1827–1833." In *Canadian*

Protestant and Catholic Missions, 1820s-1960s: Historical Essays in Honour of John Webster Grant, edited by John S. Moir and C. T. McIntire, 23–74. New York: Peter Lang, 1988.

Mulvey, Mary Doris, O.P. *French Catholic Missionaries in the Present United States, 1604–1791*. Catholic University of America Studies in Church History, no. 23. Washington, D.C.: Catholic University, 1936.

Nicks, John. "David Thompson." In *Dictionary of Canadian Biography*, edited by Francess G. Halpenny, 8:878–84. Toronto: University of Toronto Press, 1985.

Norton, Sr. Mary Aquinas. *Catholic Missionary Activities in the Northwest, 1818–1864*. Washington, D.C.: Catholic University, 1930.

Parker, Seymour. "The Wiitiko Psychosis in the Context of Ojibwa Personality and Culture." *American Anthropologist* 62 (1960): 603–23.

Peers, Laura L. "Rich Man, Poor Man, Beggarman, Chief: Saulteaux in the Red River Settlement." In *Papers of the Eighteenth Algonquian Conference*, edited by William Cowan, 261–70. Ottawa: Carleton University Press, 1987.

Perry, Richard J. "The Fur Trade and the Status of Women in the Western Subarctic." *Ethnohistory* 26, no. 4 (1979): 363–75.

Peterson, Jacqueline. "Ethnogenesis: The Settlement and Growth of a 'New People' in the Great Lakes Region, 1702–1815." In *An Anthology of Western Great Lakes Indian History*, edited by Donald L. Fixico, 111–77. Milwaukee: University of Wisconsin Press, 1987.

————. "The People in Between: Indian-White Marriage and the Genesis of a Métis Society and Culture in the Great Lakes Region, 1680–1830." Ph.D. diss., University of Illinois at Chicago Circle, 1981.

Rauschenbush, Walter. "Conceptions of Missions." In *The Social Gospel in America, 1880–1920*, edited by Robert T. Handy, 268–73. New York: Oxford University Press, 1966.

Ray, Arthur J. *Indians in the Fur Trade: Their Role as Trappers, Hunters, and Middlemen in the Lands Southwest of Hudson Bay, 1660–1870*. Toronto: University of Toronto Press, 1974.

Rezek, Rev. Antoine Ivan. *History of the Diocese of Sault Ste. Marie and Marquette . . . .* 2 vols. Houghton, Mich.: N.p., 1907.

Rhodes, Richard A., and Evelyn M. Todd. "Subarctic Algonquian Languages." In *Handbook of North American Indians*, vol. 6: *Subarctic*, edited by June Helm, 52–66. Washington, D.C.: Smithsonian Institution, 1981.

Ritzenthaler, Robert E. "Southwestern Chippewa." In *Handbook of North American Indians*, vol. 15: *Northeast*, edited by Bruce E. Trigger, 743–59. Washington, D.C.: Smithsonian Institution, 1978.

Rogers, Edward S. "Cultural Adaptations: The Northern Ojibwa of the Boreal Forest, 1670–1890." In *Boreal Forest Adaptations: The Northern Algonkians*, edited by A. Theodore Steegmann, Jr., 85–142. New York: Plenum Press, 1983.

————. "The Mistassini Cree." In *Hunters and Gatherers Today: A Socioeconomic Study of Eleven Such Cultures in the Twentieth Century*, edited by M. G. Bicchiere, 90–137. New York: Holt, Rinehart & Winston, 1972.

————. "Southeastern Chippewa." In *Handbook of North American Indians*, vol. 15: *Northeast*, edited by Bruce E. Trigger, 760–71. Washington, D.C.: Smithsonian Institution, 1978.

Rogers, Edward S., and James G. E. Smith. "Environment and Culture in the Shield and Mackenzie Borderlands." In *Handbook of North American Indians*, vol. 6: *Subarctic*, edited by June Helm, 130–45. Washington, D.C.: Smithsonian Institution, 1981.

Rohrl, Vivian J. "A Nutritional Factor in Windigo Psychosis." *American Anthropologist* 72 (1970): 97–101.

Rohrlich-Leavitt, Ruby, Barbara Sykes, and Elizabeth Weatherford. "Aboriginal Women: Male and Female Anthropological Perspectives." In *Toward an Anthropology of Women*, edited by Rayna R. Reiter, 110–26. New York: Monthly Review Press, 1975.

Ronda, James. "The European Indian: Jesuit Civilization Planning in New France." *Church History* 41, no. 3 (1972): 385–95.

————. " 'We Are Well As We Are': An Indian Critique of Seventeenth-Century Christian Missions." *William and Mary Quarterly* 24, no. 1 (1977): 66–82.

Rosaldo, Michelle Zimbalist. "Women, Culture, and Society: A Theoretical Overview." In *Woman, Culture, and Society*, edited by Michelle Zimbalist Rosaldo and Louise Lamphere, 17–42. Stanford: Stanford University Press, 1974.

Roy, Andrew T. "Overseas Mission Policies—An Historical Overview." *Journal of Presbyterian History* 57, no. 3 (1979): 186–228.

Sacks, Karen. "Engels Revisited: Women, the Organization of Production, and Private Property." In *Toward an Anthropology of Women*, edited by Rayna R. Reiter, 211–34. New York: Monthly Review Press, 1975.

Sanday, Peggy R. "Female Status in the Public Domain." In *Woman, Culture, and Society*, edited by Michelle Zimbalist Rosaldo and

Louise Lamphere, 189–206. Stanford: Stanford University Press, 1974.

Service, Elman R. *Primitive Social Organization: An Evolutionary Perspective.* New York: Random House, 1962.

Shea, John Dawson Gilmary. *History of the Catholic Missions Among the Indian Tribes of the United States, 1529–1854.* New York: E. Dunnigan, 1855.

Shepardson, Mary. "The Status of Navajo Women." *American Indian Quarterly* 6 (1982): 149–69.

Singleton, Gregory H. "Protestant Voluntary Organizations and the Shaping of Victorian America." *American Quarterly* 27, no. 2 (1975): 549–60.

Slosser, Gaius Jackson. "Walter Lowrie, Mission Organizer." *Journal of the Presbyterian Historical Society* 36 (1958): 3–18.

Smith, Donald B. *Sacred Feathers: The Reverend Peter Jones (Kahkewaquonaby) and the Mississauga Indians.* Toronto: University of Toronto Press, 1987.

Smith, Timothy L. *Revivalism and Social Reform: American Protestantism on the Eve of the Civil War.* Baltimore: Johns Hopkins University Press, 1980.

Smith-Rosenberg, Carroll, and Charles Rosenberg. "The Female Animal: Medical and Biological Views of Woman and Her Role in Nineteenth-Century America." *Journal of American History* 60 (1973): 332–56.

Speck, Frank G. *Naskapi: The Savage Hunters of the Labrador Peninsula.* Norman: University of Oklahoma Press, 1935.

Spindler, Louise S. *Menomini Women and Culture Change.* American Anthropological Association Memoir no. 91. Menasha, Wis.: American Anthropological Association, 1962.

Spindler, Louise, and George Spindler. "Male and Female Adaptations in Culture Change." *American Anthropologist* 60 (1958): 217–33.

Stage, Sarah. *Female Complaints: Lydia Pinkham and the Business of Women's Medicine.* New York: Norton, 1979.

Steinbring, Jack H. "Saulteaux of Lake Winnipeg." In *Handbook of North American Indians*, vol. 6: *Subarctic*, edited by June Helm, 244–55. Washington, D.C.: Smithsonian Institution, 1981.

Stocking, George W., Jr. *Race, Culture, and Evolution: Essays in the History of Anthropology.* New York: Free Press, 1968.

Stone, Lyle M., and Donald Chaput. "History of the Upper Great Lakes Area." In *Handbook of North American Indians*, vol. 15: *Northeast*, edited by Bruce G. Trigger, 602–9. Washington, D.C.: Smithsonian Institution, 1978.

Sutherland, Rev. Alexander. "The Methodist Church in Relation to Missions." In *Centennial of Canadian Methodism*, 253–72. Toronto: William Briggs, 1891.

Tanner, Adrian. *Bringing Home Animals: Religious Ideology and Mode of Production of the Mistassini Cree Hunters*. Social and Economic Studies, no. 23. [St. John's,] Newfoundland: Institute of Social and Economic Research, Memorial University of Newfoundland, 1979.

Teicher, Morton I. *Windigo Psychosis: A Study of a Relationship Between Belief and Behavior Among the Indians of Northeastern Canada*. New York: AMS Press, 1985.

Thistle, Paul C. *Indian-European Trade Relations in the Lower Saskatchewan River Region to 1840*. Winnipeg: University of Manitoba Press, 1986.

Thompson, E. P. *The Making of the English Working Class*. New York: Vintage Books, 1966.

Tiffany, Sharon W. "Introduction: Theoretical Issues in the Anthropological Study of Women." In *Women and Society: An Anthropological Reader*, edited by Sharon W. Tiffany, 1–35. St. Albans, Vt.: Eden Press Women's Publications, 1979.

Trigger, Bruce G. "American Archaeology as Native History: A Review Essay." *William and Mary Quarterly* 40 (1983): 413–52.

——— . *The Children of Aataentsic: A History of the Huron People to 1660*. 2 vols. Montreal: McGill-Queen's University Press, 1976.

Van Kirk, Sylvia. *"Many Tender Ties": Women in Fur-Trade Society, 1670–1870*. Winnipeg: Watson & Dwyer, 1980.

Vecsey, Christopher. *Traditional Ojibwa Religion and Its Historical Changes*. Philadelphia: American Philosophical Society, 1983.

Vernon, Walter N., and Ruth M. Vernon. "Indian Missions of North America." In *Encyclopedia of World Methodism*, edited by Nolan B. Harmon, 1211. Nashville: United Methodist Publishing House, 1974.

Verwyst, P. Chrysostomus, O.F.M. *Life and Labors of Rt. Rev. Frederic Baraga, First Bishop of Marquette, Mich., to Which Are Added Short Sketches of the Lives and Labor of Other Indian Missionaries of the Northwest*. Milwaukee: M. H. Wiltzius, 1900.

Vizenor, Gerald. *The People Named the Chippewa: Narrative Histories*. Minneapolis: University of Minnesota Press, 1984.

Welter, Barbara. "The Cult of True Womanhood: 1820–1860." *American Quarterly* 18 (1966): 151–74.

——— . "She Hath Done What She Could: Protestant Women's Missionary Careers in Nineteenth-Century America." *American Quarterly* 30 (1978): 624–38.

Williams, Norman James. "Abishabis the Cree." *Studies in Religion/ Sciences religieuses* 9, no. 2 (1980): 217–45.

Wright, Mary C. "Economic Development and Native American Women in the Early Nineteenth Century." *American Quarterly* 33 (1981): 525–36.

Index

Compositor:	BookMasters, Inc.
Text:	11/13 Baskerville
Display:	Baskerville
Printer:	Braun-Brumfield, Inc.
Binder:	Braun-Brumfield, Inc.